Nativity scenes ⋯ ⋯ ⋯ *s*
always stirs the ⋯ **D0608645** ⋯ *e*
readers with refle ⋯ ⋯ *surrounded the birth of Jesus, not the caricatures of popular fantasy. With a mixture of expository insight, historical background and psychological sensitivity, he brings the characters to life. And not just the obvious ones such as Mary, Joseph, the shepherds and kings. We are also introduced to the emperor Augustus, Simeon, the narrators themselves, Matthew and Luke and of course John the Baptist and his parents. A lively read that warms the heart and offers a fresh and challenging angle from which to view familiar stories.*

Chris Wright,
International Ministry Director,
The Langham Partnership International

Familiar with the Christmas story? Maybe. But we can miss the extraordinary human drama that surrounds the most remarkable event this world has yet witnessed. With well chosen historical sketches, careful explanation of the Gospel accounts, and imaginative yet plausible story-telling, Tom Houston sets the scene for Christ's birth by truly getting into the shoes of the diverse human actors drawn into that drama.

We feel their emotions, identify with their reactions, and marvel at the way personal details as well as great political movements all combine to demonstrate God's sovereign control. With pertinent application to our lives today, this book will be of relevance to Christians of all ages.

Jonathan Lamb,
Associate General Secretary, IFES

To most of us the characters in the story of Jesus' birth are somewhat remote and unreal. We may know them as overfamiliar players in a children's Christmas pageant, loveable and a bit laughable, with towelled turbans on their small heads. Or they may seem remote figures from a long-ago time and faraway place that are a piece of ancient history. In any case they may seem unrelated to our real lives.

*Most of us also know the names of only the major players —
Mary and Joseph, the wise men, the shepherds, but little about
the other characters. Now Tom Houston has given us a
remarkable and helpful study. With careful research and a
sensitive imagination he introduces us in a fresh way to a cast
of real people, people like us, with real feelings of joy and fear
and jealousy and longing, who lived in a real time and place.
Read Characters Around the Cradle and Christmas will live
for you in a new way. Perhaps as never before you will realize
that the Christmas story was a real happening that can make
a difference in your real life today!*

**Leighton Ford
President, Leighton Ford Ministries,
Charlotte, North Carolina USA**

*Tom Houston writes as he notes — with tenacity and fervor.
The simple truth is that Tom grabs hold of the characters
that he paints, he dissects them, he examines them, and he
puts them back together again with a clarity of thought that
makes them spring to life 2000 years after the time that they
walked this earth.*

*In the same way he grabs hold of the reader. It's hard to
put this book down, because the imagination is charged by
the stark reality of the characters portrayed.*

*Yet this is no mechanical exercise. It's not a historical
reflection. What Tom Houston does is to give fresh insight
and new understanding for today's reader.*

*This is what Tom has always done. He explores the
character with which he is dealing, and then he fires the
imagination and captures the response of the reader so that
we want to learn, to grow, and to copy the example that
he's given.*

*It would be hard to read these words without being
changed, for all Tom has done is bring Scripture to life, in
order that the Holy Spirit may teach us today what it truly
means.*

**Dr Clive Calver
President, World Relief**

Characters Around the Cradle

Witnesses to the greatest story ever told

Tom Houston

Christian Focus

Dedication

To my mother,
Mary Houston,
whose support and self-sacrifice
gave me a start in life and in Christian
service that I value more than I can express.

© Tom Houston 2002

ISBN 1 85792 755 9

Published in 2002 by
Christian Focus Publications, Geanies House, Fearn,
Tain, Ross-shire, IV20 1TW, Scotland

www.christianfocus.com

Cover design by Alister MacInnes

Printed and bound by
Cox & Wyman, Reading, Berkshire

Contents

PART TWO

Introduction

Christmas makes people both happy and frustrated, especially Christian people. There is a tug of war between the secular Christmas with its tinsel, glitter and high spending on gifts, and the meaning it was supposed to have from the unusual birth of Jesus. This book is intended to give people a more rounded and detailed picture of the realities of the Christmas story, by looking at how the original events affected the people involved.

Assumptions

I start from the assumption that there was a real connected story spread over a specific period of time and located in real geographical places. This is not immediately apparent in the gospels, so, I have used my imagination to supply the links that make it a continuous story, keeping true to what the gospels say. On their human side, I assume that the gospels were produced and preserved by competent people who were at least as intelligent and devout as we are today. I assume that they were quite capable of accurately interpreting their own experience and of presenting what they had seen, heard and read in the language of their readers. I believe that we can gain an adequate understanding of what they say if we work at it.

I assume also that God was willing and able to arrange for the gospels' records of Jesus, to be written and be preserved in ways that would achieve his purposes for them among people everywhere who want to know about Jesus. Those who believe in God will be untroubled by this, for they assume that he would not, and did not, leave his message to humankind in a form that can only be understood by a handful of professional scholars, who cannot even agree among themselves on what the message is.

The events are basically a piece of history. When Luke came to research them, he had to find and evaluate the documents, interview the right people and shape his material for his intended readers like any historian (Luke 1:1–4). It was no different with Matthew. The kind of people that Luke and Matthew were, shines through in the selection and presentation of their material. Equally, the particular values and emphases, that were important to them and their audiences, can be seen in the way their material is presented.

It is clear from the many references the writers make to the Holy Spirit in the text that they thought he was superintending the events and the composite recording of them that we have in the gospels. As a result, these are both the words of men and the Word of God, introducing us to the most significant happening in history up to that time. We call it the incarnation, when the Son of God became a human being to undertake the task of recovering the world from the mess in which it had put itself by its wilfulness.

The stories surrounding Jesus' birth make up an interlocking chain of revelatory events. They start with the unusual birth of John the Baptist and move right through to the man he became. The point to which Matthew and Luke are moving us is the beginning of the ministry of Jesus himself (Matt. 4:12). This is recognized in church lectionaries for Advent which use Scriptures about John the Baptist both before and after Christmas. I have therefore included six chapters on the short life and work of the adult John the Baptist.

In all these events, there are supernatural interventions. Angels appear directly and in dreams. There is a dream without an angel and several remarkable coincidences of timing. There is a voice from heaven. It was through these that the revelations were given or confirmed.

Angels
I personally have no experience of angels and I seldom have dreams that I can recall. I am impressed, however, by the way in which both

dreams and angels are used in the Bible when God wishes to communicate with people.

Angels have been present since creation and throughout the Bible they are seen to be involved in God's plans for the world. They closed the garden of Eden, protected Lot, saved Hagar and her child and stayed Abraham's hand from sacrificing his son. They communicated the law to Moses, led the people of God through the desert. They announced births and callings and assisted the prophets, just to cite a few examples.

Finally, the angel Gabriel announced the birth of the forerunner, John the Baptist and that of Jesus himself. Angels sang praises at the birth of Christ: 'Glory to God in the highest!' They protected Jesus in his infancy and served him after his temptations in the desert. They strengthened him in his agony in the garden, when he could have been saved by them from the hands of his enemies. It was angels who proclaimed the Good News of Christ's Resurrection and they will be present at Christ's return.

Dreams

Abraham Lincoln said, 'How much there is in the Bible about dreams! There are, I think, some 16 chapters in the Old Testament and four or five in the New in which dreams are mentioned; and there are many other passages scattered throughout the book which refer to visions. If we believe the Bible, we must accept the fact that, in the old days, God and his angels came to men in their sleep and made themselves known in dreams.' Lincoln was discussing a disturbing dream he had, talking with a group of friends just before his assassination. He went on to say that, after the dream in which he saw his own body lying in state in the White House, he had opened up his Bible, and 'strange as it may appear, it was the 28th chapter of Genesis, which relates the wonderful dream Jacob had. I turned to other passages, and seemed to encounter a dream or a vision wherever I looked. I kept on turning the leaves of the old book, and everywhere my eyes fell upon passages recording matters strangely in keeping with my own thoughts – supernatural visitations, dreams, visions, and so forth.'

Coincidences

Miracles are often seen to be so, because of their timing. Thunder and lightning and heavy rain are common place. The miracle was that they appeared just at the time Elijah was praying for rain (1 Kings 18:41–45). In the accounts of the birth of Jesus, timing was critical to Mary and Elizabeth, confirming the message that the angel had brought to them.

God was at work in the story we are about

to trace. He was working for the benefit of humankind and so, for my benefit and that of my readers.

Tom Houston
Oxford

PART ONE

1

Herod and his Temple

Official Religion

The story of the events surrounding the birth of Jesus begins with the words, 'During the time when Herod was king of Judea, there was a priest.. doing his work... in the Temple' (Luke 1:5).

Herod's Temple

This was a Temple that Herod himself had built. He was a great builder. He was a benefactor and builder of public works on a grand scale. In honour of Caesar, he transformed the town of Samaria and called it 'Sebaste' which is Greek for 'Augustus'. At the coast, he built Caesarea with a large port. It became the Roman capital of Palestine. Paul stood trial there before the Governor Felix and King Agrippa (Acts 24–26).

The most brilliant period of Herod's reign was from 25 to 14BC (age 48–59). He devoted himself, just like the rulers who followed Alexander the Great, to the erection of magnificent buildings in many towns of his kingdom. He also built temples to the Emperor, Augustus, who people had begun to say was a god. He changed the face of Jerusalem, beautifying the city with new buildings in the current Hellenistic style. There were theatres, amphitheatres and a hippodrome for horse and chariot races. In honour of his friend the emperor, he also instituted games every five years, with athletes, gladiators and wild animals participating. About the year 24BC he erected his own, imposing royal palace, as celebrated for the luxury of its furnishings as for the strength of its three impregnable towers.

But the Jews in Jerusalem were ashamed of their Temple. This centre of their national life, was built originally by Solomon. It was destroyed by Nebuchadnezzar and all its treasures carried away with the people to Babylon. It lay in ruins for nearly a hundred years. When the people came back from exile they built it again. The story is in the book of Ezra. It was called The Second Temple and it was a much inferior building to the one built by Solomon. In the centuries that followed, Jerusalem changed hands many times and nearly every time more damage was done to The Second Temple.

Herod's fine new buildings going up all around it, made it look totally insignificant.

It was a real stroke of genius on the part of Herod, who was not even a real Jew, to put all his resources at the service of the deep-seated longings of the chosen people. He drew up and announced his impressive plan to replace the dilapidated Second Temple built after the exile. The building he planned would be a temple larger and more beautiful than even the Temple of Solomon itself.

He showed his respect for the prescriptions of the Law of Moses in the process of its construction. Ten thousand workmen prepared the stones off site, in advance. One thousand priests were trained as masons at his expense. In those parts of the Temple where only a priest could set foot, the priests were to demolish the old building, stone by stone, and gradually rebuild it with the prepared materials, without interrupting the ceremonies for a single day. Work took 18 months on the sanctuary itself, and eight years on the courtyards and porticoes. We learn from the Gospel of St John that 40 years later the work was still in progress (John 2:20). It was completed only in AD63.

It covered double the area of the Second Temple which it replaced. One person familiar with the details has said, 'It is almost impossible to realize the effect which would be produced by a building, itself longer and higher than the greatest Cathedral, standing on a solid mass of masonry at the top of a hill with a sheer drop on the eastern side'. The dazzling whiteness of stone, fresh from the masons' hands, bathed in sunlight made it one of the wonders of the world at that time. Yet it only stood eight years after it was finally completed.

In the sanctuary of this magnificent building the opening scene of the drama of the birth of Jesus took place when the priest Zechariah was working there.

Herod's Early Life

Herod had been King for more than 30 years. The way he became king would have earned him the title of 'the come-back kid' in his day. It is not for nothing he was called Herod the Great. Herod, like his father, was an Idumean, what we would call an Arab. Julius Caesar made his father Governor of the Roman province of Judea in 47BC. Herod and his father qualified as Jews only because a ruling High Priest of the Jews, Hyrcanus I, had conquered their country, Idumea, and forcibly converted them to Judaism and ordered the men to be circumcised.

Herod's education had consisted of being taken around with his father in the violent and troubled days of the Roman Civil Wars. He became familiar with military camps and royal courts and learned his political flair by watching his father. It was from his mother, however, that he inherited his impetuous character. In his mid- twenties, his father gave him Galilee to govern and some armies to lead.

Julius Caesar was assassinated in 44BC and another civil war broke out. His father lost his Roman patron. Serving the Romans during their civil wars was not easy in any part of their vast territories, especially in the Middle East. You had to be something of an acrobat to stay upright and hold on to what you had when the sides changed so quickly. Herod had climbed the ranks of being a prince, a governor of Galilee and a general. By 42BC he was reduced to being a fugitive. He was utterly alone. No one would rally to him. As a Ghanaian student once said to me about African leaders, it was 'from grace to grass'.

He had no friends left except in Rome and Rome was a long way off. But he decided to go there. He went from Jericho, via Egypt and in a ship given to him by Cleopatra. Herod was a favourite of Mark Antony who was ten years older than him. Through his influence Herod was made King of Judea in 40BC by the Roman Senate. This was the historical event on which Jesus based his parable of the pounds. 'There was once a man of high rank who was going to a country far away to be made king, after which he planned to come back home. Before he left, he called his ten servants and gave them each a gold coin and told them, "See

what you can earn with this while I am gone'"
(Luke 19:12). It took three years and a lot of
scheming and fighting before Herod captured
Jerusalem (37BC) and began an illustrious reign.

Herod's Reign

Soon after he took Jerusalem, Herod executed
more than 40 of the 72 members of the
Sanhedrin or Council of Jewish Leaders. He
made sure that body did what he said and kept
itself strictly to religious matters. As a 'client
king', Herod strode out of the Roman Senate
as King of the Jews, with Mark Antony on
one arm and Octavian on the other. Octavian
was to become Caesar Augustus just 13 years
later. Herod was allowed to rule Judea on
behalf of the Romans. He was able to keep
out Roman ex-soldiers, settlers, administrators,
tax collectors, etc. It was not until ten years
after his death that Judea was made a Roman
Province and all these Roman functionaries, that
we meet in the pages of the gospels, came in.

There had been no real King of the Jews
for five and a half centuries since Jehoiachin
(Matt. 1:11). Judea had been subject to a
succession of different great powers, and had
experienced different arrangements for the
government of the country. The most regular
was that the High Priest of the time was also
made the civil power. The position of High
Priest had usually been for life but Herod

changed that. He appointed and deposed High Priests as he pleased, sometimes in quick succession. He even kept the ornamental robes of the High Priest under lock and key, in his own palace, only releasing them to be worn at festivals. It was important to Herod that religion should serve the interests of the state.

The 'Chief Priests' that we know only in the New Testament, came into being as a consequence of this policy. It included the present and past High Priests, many of whom were from the same family. The first ever mention of them is when Herod summoned them to meet and inform him where Messiah was to be born (Matt. 2:4).

An Attractive Person

Herod was said to be tall, handsome, with great charm and an expert in the field of public relations. He was athletic, capable of feats of great endurance, a fine horseman, expert wrestler, first-class shot with the bow. He had dark hair, a golden complexion, thin sensitive lips, a delicately moulded nose, small crisp ears, large liquid eyes, fern-like lashes, beneath sable eyebrows, and he had instinctive knowledge of other men's faults. A friend of the Jews at home and abroad in the Diaspora, he was the perfect diplomat.

A Consummate Diplomatist

One of the most remarkable meetings in history must have been Cleopatra's visit to Herod in Jerusalem in 34BC. He told the rather unlikely story afterwards that she had tried to make love to him. He went on to say that he had thought of having her murdered but then decided that he had better not, so she survived, but not for as long as Herod did. After her death, Augustus gave Herod some of her territory, extending the borders of Judea. No Jew since Solomon reigned over so great a kingdom.

How does a small power reconcile its own special, peculiar way of life with a sufficient degree of conformity required by a super power? Herod's ambition was to keep Judea intact, as peaceful and as prosperous a country as it was capable of becoming, in a world dominated by a Western power – Rome. He had to be Jew enough to retain control of his Jewish subjects; pro-Roman enough to preserve the confidence of Rome; and Greek enough to impress his numerous non-Jewish neighbours. While he lived, he did very great things for Romans, Greeks and Jews alike. He was Arab by race, a Roman by political allegiance, a Greek by culture.

How much this was a triumph is shown by the fact that it is said that he was loved by Caesar Augustus next only to Agrippa,

Caesar's second in command and loved by Agrippa next only to Caesar Augustus.

An Able Administrator

Apart from small groups of ruined noblemen and Messianic revolutionaries, the Jews never had it so good. He spent gigantic sums of money with such efficiency that without an oppressive system of taxation he left the country rich. The ordinary peasants, merchants and citizenry were prospering and knew it. Herod's' mighty public works had given full employment and had eliminated social agitation. When complaints broke out after his death, Nicolas of Damascus, his biographer, was quick to point out that there had been no sign of them when he was alive. He brought the Kingdom peace that lasted with only minor and peripheral exceptions for the entire 33 years of his reign. It was a peace free from the incursions of Roman officials. Herod was the face of the Roman Peace (*Pax Romana*) to the Jews.

Herod's Motives

For Herod, building the Temple was not a religious act. He was playing the religious card to achieve his personal goals. It is common enough for rulers to use religion. A notorious example was what Stalin did when he was confronted with the need to fight the Germans in World War II. In his first speech after the German invasion on 3 July 1941, he began, 'Comrades, citizens, *brothers and sisters'*. The Christian form of address had resurfaced from his seminary days. Only three years previously he had proclaimed a 'Godless Five-Year Plan,' by the end of which (in 1943) the last church was to be closed and the last priest destroyed.

It came to his attention that Ilya, Metropolitan of the Lebanon Mountains, had shut himself up in an underground cell and gone without food or sleep while he knelt in prayer for Russia to the Virgin Mary. He had a miraculous vision, which he described in a letter to the leaders of the Orthodox Church in Russia. On the third day the Virgin Mary had appeared to him in a pillar of fire and had given him God's sentence: 'The churches and monasteries must be reopened throughout the country. Priests must be brought back from imprisonment, Leningrad must not be surrendered, but the sacred icon of Our Lady of Kazan should be carried around the city boundary, taken on to Moscow, where a service should be held, and thence to Stalingrad.'

Stalin decided to act on Metropolitan Ilya's vision. On his orders many priests were brought back from the camps. In Leningrad, besieged by the Germans and gradually dying of hunger, the inhabitants were astounded, and uplifted, to see the wonder-working icon of Our Lady of Kazan brought out into the streets and borne in procession. From Leningrad the icon went to Moscow, and was then sent to besieged Stalingrad. It was displayed in each of the three great cities which had not surrendered to the enemy. Twenty thousand churches were reopened. He and his generals sent troops into battle with the words 'God go with you'. On 17 October *Pravda* reported that the head of the Bolshevik Party had met the interim head of the Patriarchate, Metropolitan Sergei, the first occasion of its kind since October 1917. In the course of their meeting, it was said, Stalin had 'reacted sympathetically to the proposal to elect a Patriarch, and said that no obstacles would be put in its way by the government.' After the war, however, Stalin returned to his characteristic repression of the churches and their leaders.

A Different Outcome
After Herod died, the Jews abandoned his policy of working with the Romans that had led to such great prosperity. In the case of Herod's Temple, the Jewish leaders took over this place of worship and made it first a lucrative business in manipulation of the Temple Tax and profits from the system of animal sacrifices. Then they made it the

symbol of Jewish nationalism. They began to plot and fight against the Romans. They resolved to fight to the death in the Temple's defence and made it the scene of perhaps the most bloody siege in history. It was destroyed, as predicted by Jesus, in the siege of Jerusalem by the Romans in AD70(Matt. 24:2). They also brought on themselves the virtual destruction of the Jewish state for 19 centuries until 1948.

Today little remains of Herod's Temple except the vast terrace surrounding the Al Aqsah Mosque and the Wailing Wall.

The Temple and the Child

This was the Temple where the angel Gabriel announced to the priest Zechariah that he and his wife would have a son, the forerunner of Messiah (Luke 1: 1–23). Here the infant Jesus was presented before the Lord and recognized as Messiah by the aged Simeon and Anna (Luke 2:22–38). The Temple and the child become symbols of two kinds of religion. One is ornate and grand and official. The other is weak and small and seemingly insignificant. One is outward and impressive. The other is inward and life-changing.

It is significant, perhaps alarming, that today the best attended services in the churches are at Christmas. The nativity scene with mother and child are brought into ornate buildings and the people flock into them.

Originally it was the opposite. To see the Christ child you had to go out into the meanest of buildings, under the cold winter stars.

The contrast and the tension keep cropping up in the life of Jesus right to the last week of his life, when he cleansed this Temple by overturning the tables of the money changers and chasing out the animals that were there for sale. He called it a den of thieves when it should have been a house of prayer for all nations (Luke 19:45–46).

The Temple figured in his trial where some witnesses charged him of threatening to destroy the Temple (Mark 14:58). 'We heard him say, "I will tear down this Temple which men have made, and after three days I will build one that is not made by men."' Even when he died on the Cross, the curtain hanging in the Temple was torn in two, from top to bottom, a symbol that there was a new way into the presence of God. (Mark 15:38).

We need to make up our minds whether we want to be Temple Christians or those who want the Christ who was born in the manger really to dwell in us, individually (2 Cor. 6:15–16), or in the fellowship of the church (1 Cor. 3:16–17). We will look at Herod again in Chapter 11.

2

Zechariah

An Old Man and his Prayers

Luke 1:5–25, 57–80

Towards the end of the reign of Herod the Great, there was a couple who lived not far from Jerusalem. Zechariah was a priest and his wife Elizabeth was also from a priestly family. Being a priest meant that they lived on, and farmed, land set aside for the priests. They also had their income supplemented by their share of the tithes and offerings that the people brought to the Temple in Jerusalem.

A Priest and his Great Moment

Like all these priests, Zechariah had to go up to the great Temple in Jerusalem three times a year to help out with the general running of the great festivals. These brought hundreds of thousands of Jews from all over the country and, in those peaceful, prosperous days, from all over the world.

He had also to be ready to be called to the

Temple for the one week of special duty twice each year that was assigned to his 'order' of about 800 priests, the order of Abijah (v.5). There were so many priests that the really sacred duties of assisting in the daily offerings only came around very occasionally. Sometimes it was only once in a lifetime. Sometimes they never had the chance at all because they were chosen by lot.

Zechariah and Elizabeth were very old, so they were as old or older than King Herod himself. They lived near Jerusalem where the king had his palace. There were about 20,000 priests in Judea at the time. Herod had not been very friendly to them. He had reason to be suspicious of the priests. For centuries the High Priest when appointed, held the post for life. In the recent past, the High Priest had been virtual head of state, in the absence of a king or Governor. When Herod was made King of the Jews in Rome, the High Priest was his main rival. To offset this potential source of trouble, Herod appointed his own nominees to the post and dismissed and appointed them at will. Those who were ex-priests under this regime, came with their families to be known as the 'Chief Priests' that we meet in the four gospels.

Priests like Zechariah did not regard Herod with favour, even if he brought the country prosperity that it had not known for a long time. Still, they were won over to some degree by the fact that among his many great building projects, his most prestigious building was the new Temple in Jerusalem. Herod courted the favour of the priests by training 1,000 of them to be masons and carpenters to work on the building. In this way there was no sacrilege committed by builders trespassing into areas reserved for consecrated priests. Zechariah would be about 50 years of age when this work began. For ten years the Temple was like a building site. Zechariah, like all other priests, had to function as best he could and control the crowds that came up for the festivals. That disruption ended three or four years before our story. Building still went on, here and there, for another 70 years, to finish off the buildings and courts on the outer perimeter of the area. It was a magnificent building, better than Solomon's and better than the Second Temple that replaced it after the exile. So, as Zechariah got older, he performed his priest's duties in very beautiful surroundings.

Zechariah and Elizabeth had one very deep sorrow. They had no children. This was a great reproach in that society and was assumed to be a kind of judgment on the couple, especially the woman. This was hard to understand because they were devout and showed their faith in God by leading exemplary lives (v.6). They kept out of trouble's way. Even more important, they kept out of Herod's way and imagined that they would see out their time in peace and quiet.

As it happened, Zechariah's big moment came round towards the end of the prosperous but cruel reign of Herod the Great. He went down very nervously to the Temple in Jerusalem to be there for the Sabbath that began his week of duty. He was chosen by lot to burn incense on the golden altar in the Holy place (v.9). He'd won the lottery in priests' terms! There was no greater honour or responsibility. He performed prescribed ablutions to make sure he was 'holy' enough to enter the holy place. He put on special, heavily adorned garments. 'So he went into the Temple of the Lord, while the crowd of people outside prayed during the hour when the incense was burnt' (vv.9–10). All went well, until he was right inside with no other person present.

A Husband and his Prayers

'An angel of the Lord appeared to him, standing on the right of the altar where the incense was burnt. When Zechariah saw him, he was alarmed and felt afraid. But the angel said to him, "Don't be afraid, Zechariah! God has heard your prayer, and your wife Elizabeth will bear you a son. You are to name him John"' (vv.11–13).

The childless man was to become a father
in his old age. His elderly wife was to become
a mother. While he was trying to come to
terms with this thunderbolt, the angel seemed
to think it could only be good news and
continued: 'How glad and happy you will be,
and how happy many others will be when he
is born! He will be a great man in the Lord's
sight' (vv.14–15).

'So the boy will grow to be a great man',
he thought, but the angel went on:

'He must not drink any wine or strong
drink. From his very birth he will be filled
with the Holy Spirit' (v.15).

'So, he is to be a Nazarite, like Samson!'
The unreality of it grew by the sentence.

'and he will bring back many of the people
of Israel to the Lord their God. He will go
ahead of the Lord, strong and mighty like the
prophet Elijah' (v.17).

'Another Elijah!', he thought. 'I know what
that means. It means the forerunner of the
Messiah! This is too much!'

'He will bring fathers and children together
again; he will turn disobedient people back to
the way of thinking of the righteous; he will
get the Lord's people ready for him' (v.17).

'That's it! It is what Malachi said, the very
words!' Unable to contain himself, he blurted
out, 'How shall I know if this is so? I am an
old man, and my wife is old also.' That was

what he said, but it seems that was not what he meant.

The angel had said, 'God has heard your prayer.' The Bible suggests that he had got used to his prayer not being answered. Things were now very comfortable. Now he did not want it answered. The Angel was messing things up and at this late stage too! How many years he had suffered the reproach that fell on him and his wife, Elizabeth, because they could not have children. He had steered his way through a bundle of emotions only known to those who have had the same experience. He felt cheated out of a precious thing he had expected like every married couple – the blessing of children. Like every childless couple, they waited every month for years, hoping against hope that Elizabeth would conceive. It put a strain on their relationship. He might even have thought of divorcing Elizabeth and marrying another woman, but their common desire to do God's will had kept them from that.

It had been difficult with the in-laws on both sides who were always asking or hinting that they were looking forward to grandchildren. They were worried, tense, irritable and deeply sad. They wondered if they were being punished for past mistakes, yet they were exemplary in their lives and their devotion to God. Sometimes it tended to undermine their trust in each other. They were successively angry, jealous of others, devalued and alienated from their friends.

They had prayed and prayed and prayed to no avail. But they had weathered all that and had come to an accommodation. They had to get on with their lives. After the menopause it was easier. They could begin to stop the monthly round of hoping and struggling. They would adjust to their situation. Now a forgotten prayer caught up with Zechariah and he did not much like the idea of his forgotten prayer being answered.

It is not unusual for us to give up on prayer. Many of us have prayers that we prayed once but we do not pray them any more. Some of them, no doubt, were foolish prayers and we even blush to remember them. C.S. Lewis said, 'If God had granted all the silly prayers I've made, where should I be now?' Some were possibly selfish and we are glad God knew us better than we knew ourselves and mercifully did not answer. Some, however, were not like that. We were on the right track but we have conveniently forgotten about them. We have begun to doubt after so many unanswered prayers. We would not be too keen on their being answered now. We were younger then. We are older now. We were committed to values then that no longer control our lifestyle now. We were in different circles then and we are more sophisticated now. It would be quite inconvenient if that prayer were resurrected and answered. It has bred in us some cynicism.

It may be, though, that if we are to fulfil the will of God for us now it will mean remembering past prayers and bringing them up to date. I do not suppose you will get an angel to jolt you awake as Zechariah did. But there may be enough in your recent musings or in events that are beginning to form a pattern to make you wonder if there are not years to be restored that the locusts have eaten. Or it may be that you would be thrilled, like Elizabeth, to know that some prayers you have prayed might yet be answered.

With Zechariah, this angel came and opened up the whole subject again. No wonder he asked, 'How shall I know if this is so? I am an old man, and my wife is old also' (v.18). Hope deferred makes the heart sick and undermines faith. Although he asked a question, he was really saying, 'I hope you are wrong!' He had this conversation inwardly as the angel spoke. This was not well received.

'I am Gabriel,' the angel answered. 'I stand in the presence of God, who sent me to speak to you and tell you this good news. But you have not believed my message, which will come true at the right time. Because you have not believed, you will be unable to speak; you will remain silent until the day my promise to you comes true' (vv.19–20).

When he heard that he was to be dumb, he tried to speak but he could not. Totally demoralized, he finished his task and stumbled to the entrance and came out into the bright sunlight.

'In the meantime the people were waiting for Zechariah and wondering why he was spending such a long time in the Temple. When he came out, he could not speak to them, and so they knew that he had seen a vision in the Temple. Unable to say a word, he made signs to them with his hands' (vv.21–22).

He disrobed and somehow managed to carry on till the end of his week of duty. 'When his period of service in the Temple was over, Zechariah went back home' (v.23). Zechariah's great moment seemed to have ended in disaster. He had lost the power of speech and hearing. And yet there was this promise that they would have a child. We can only imagine how he managed to get home and convey to his wife, Elizabeth, what had happened in the Temple. It is not hard to envisage how he managed to cope with his loss of speech and hearing, at home and with the neighbours in his village. Everything had to be by signs or on a slate or in the dust, with a stick or his finger.

A Child and his Role

'Some time later his wife, Elizabeth, became pregnant and did not leave the house for five months. Now at last the Lord has helped me,' she said. 'He has taken away my public disgrace!' (vv.24–25).

Then, in the sixth month of the pregnancy, a relative of theirs from up north in Nazareth arrived with another even stranger story, as he learned later. This cousin who was little more than a girl had also had a visit from the same angel, Gabriel. She too was to have a child — without even having a husband. When she came through the door and before anything more than a greeting was exchanged, his wife, Elizabeth, 'was filled with the Holy Spirit and said in a loud voice, "You are the most blessed of all women, and blessed is the child you will bear! Why should this great thing happen to me, that my Lord's mother comes to visit me? For as soon as I heard your greeting, the baby within me jumped with gladness. How happy you are to believe that the Lord's message to you will come true!"' (vv.43–45)

Clearly, Zechariah saw that his wife, Elizabeth, had recognized that what Gabriel had said to him about the Lord, who was to come, was being fulfilled in this pregnant young cousin. Then inspiration seemed to come on the young cousin and she uttered a song of praise and gratitude that, when

Zechariah learned the words, he knew it was like great songs in their past history.

Three months Mary stayed and the old woman and the young woman talked and talked and seemed to Zechariah to be alternately ecstatically happy and deeply thoughtful. He got such news reported to him as Elizabeth was able to write or sign for him.

'When the time came for Elizabeth to have her baby, she gave birth to a son. Her neighbours and relatives heard how wonderfully good the Lord had been to her, and they all rejoiced with her' (vv.57–58). So far, so good! Zechariah did what he could to help and enter into the general merriment.

'When the baby was a week old, however, they came to circumcise him, and they were going to name him Zechariah, after his father. But his mother said, 'No! His name is to be John' (vv.59–60). Zechariah was relieved as he lip read the conversation. But the neighbours were not easily put off. 'They said to her, "But you have no relatives with that name!" Then they made signs to his father, asking him what name he would like the boy to have. Zechariah asked for a writing tablet and wrote, "His name is John". How surprised they all were! At that moment Zechariah was able to speak again, and he started praising God. The neighbours were all filled with fear, and the news about these things spread through all the hill country of Judea. Everyone who heard of it thought about it and asked, "What is this child going to be? For it was plain that the Lord's power was upon him"' (vv.61–66).

The Change in the Old Man

Zechariah had realized how blessed he had been before he lost faculties that he, and we all, take for granted. I wonder if he was a talkative man, the kind of person who has a need to talk; the kind of person who is not so good at listening, who moves the conversation back always to what is going on in their head wherever the conversation of others may be intending. Was he domineering, the kind who can out-talk anyone and get the last word. If so, he had plenty of time to recognize and learn his mistake. James tells us that we are to be slow to talk and swift to listen (James 1:19). The proverb has it that the more you talk, the more likely you are to sin (Proverbs 10:19).

Zechariah was done with fear and all the inhibited behaviour that he had endured being deaf and dumb for nine months or more. He was cured of his cynicism. He was now ready to have this child, however inconvenient it would be to an old man like him, settled in his ways. Gabriel had said that 'He will bring fathers and children together again' (v.17). It is interesting that there is no place in the record about his son, John the Baptist, that relates to this prophecy. Could it be that this was primarily to be fulfilled in Zechariah himself? To him, John, to begin with, had been an unwanted child. Now that had changed. The child was very much wanted and would be called John as the angel had said. So he had to start all over again and think how the generation thought that were two removed from him and his wife. That is really asking something for an old man who thought he had left all that behind him and he could see out his time in the comfort of his own prejudices and preferences.

The generation gap is still there and it needs to be bridged if respect is to be restored and if there is to be peace and understanding in our societies. We cannot give up on that. It needs to be bridged from both ends but it is clear that the initiative needs to come most from us older people. We are the ones who are supposed to be wise. Then we need to show it and start building our end of the needed bridge.

Zechariah's turn came to be filled with the Holy Spirit and he blasted out his own prophecy that had been building up in him all that time. First things first, he spoke about the other child still being carried by their cousin from Galilee. He was the important one. He was great David's greater son. He was to show that God had remembered his covenant with their ancestor Abraham. He would bring in a new day and redeem and save them from their enemies as all their prophets had foretold (vv.67–75).

Only after that, did he speak about the baby in Elizabeth's arms in front of them all. His child would be an extraordinary prophet of God preparing the way for the Messiah who was soon to appear. When it all happened it would be like dawn after a dark, dark night. Life would take on a different quality because God had shown his mercy and kindness to them and to the world.

Zechariah became more positive than he had been for a long time. He was full of gratitude for all that had happened to him and all that it had started for his people. That is one of the best things that we who are older can do. Stop complaining because our comfort is not preserved intact. Show gratitude and appreciation for all that happens to us and always be expressing a vote of confidence in what the younger generations are going to be able to do. We become unhappy and others are bored with us if in our riper years we find a self-centredness that would never have been thought possible in us in our earlier years. May God help us to compose our own versions of Zechariah's Benedictus and boost the confidence of the latter-day 'Johns' who often feel that they are unwanted. Let us be sure that they do not get that impression from us.

3

Elizabeth

The Believing Wife

Luke 1:5–7, 23–25, 39–45

The Priest's Wife

Elizabeth's story was Zechariah's story and yet it was very different from her husband's. They both came from priestly stock. Most of the guests at their wedding were from their priestly relatives. Their married life had begun like any married life. Then it began to look as though they were not going to have children as quickly as their relatives in the extended family. As a couple, they were beginning to feel different. When all the family came together for the Passover feast, all the children participated in the Seder and then ran around looking for their special reward that Grandpa had hidden. None of the children were theirs. It emphasized their own sense of emptiness.

The endless hints from the parents on both sides, the sly glances from friends of their own generation, made them feel desolate. After all it was not their fault. They could not help it if Elizabeth did not get pregnant. They had the monthly watching and waiting to see if it had happened and always tears. They were so frustrated. Their childlessness confronted them like an enormous brick wall that they could not get through or round or over. Their sense of loss was overwhelming at times.

It led to arguments between them. Zechariah blamed Elizabeth, for in that culture it was always the woman who was at fault. It seemed to rob life of its meaning, for the whole purpose of marriage was to continue the line and pass down the blessings of the family. Zechariah felt cheated. Elizabeth felt deserted by God.

It was specially difficult when Zechariah had to go up to Jerusalem to do his priestly duty. At the festivals when Elizabeth went with him they seemed to stick out like a sore thumb on the road and in the streets of Jerusalem for everyone else had children tearing around. When he went on his own for the duties that belonged to his own group of priests, she was left behind and did not even have him for company to compensate for the lack of children. With their childlessness disappeared the secret hope of every Jewish woman, that she might be the mother of Messiah. So it went on for years, and they stuck by each other as best they could. People saw them as righteous and blameless, obeying fully all God's laws and commands (v.6).

Somewhere it began to be different. It would probably be after the menopause, when Zechariah was able to say, 'Well that's that! It is not going to happen now. We have to get on with our lives!' He began to orient himself to a life without children. He would be the best priest he could be.

It was different for Elizabeth. She recalled times in the past when God had come to couples and they had children late, like Rachel the wife of Jacob and mother of Joseph (Gen. 30:22) or Hannah the wife of Elkanah (1 Sam. 1:19–20). There were others to whom God was gracious long after the child-bearing years, like Abraham and Sarah the parents of Isaac (Gen. 21:1–2) and Manoah and his wife the parents of Samson (Judges 13:24). The flame of her faith still burned even if it was a very small flame that no one knew about but herself. Like Abraham, she hoped against hope for a child (Romans 4:18).

The Stricken Priest

Zechariah had gone down to do duty at the temple, as he did, when his group's turn came round. Elizabeth went about her business as was her habit. When the day came that her husband was due to return, she prepared their home and the meal that she knew he would like. She watched out for his arrival.

As soon as she saw him, she sensed there was something wrong. There was a man with him, obviously taking care of him, and yet neither of them spoke as they walked along. At length he came into the house and he could only gesture with exasperation written all over his face. She could see that he was unable to speak. When she spoke to him, it was obvious also that he could not hear.

His companion explained what he knew. He spoke of the tremendous privilege Zechariah had been given of drawing the lot to burn incense on the altar of incense and how pleased he had been. So he had prepared meticulously on the day and gone in alone through the curtain into the Holy Place. A crowd of worshippers waited outside. He was inside a very long time, much longer than usual. The people became impatient and then a bit anxious.

When he did come out he had staggered out gesticulating with his arms and hands. No sound came from his lips although he was obviously trying to speak. Eventually it became clear that he had lost the power of speech and hearing. The people began to speculate that perhaps he had seen a vision (v.22).

He was helped back to the priests' quarters and when he was calmed down enough they gave him a slate and he wrote a few words to explain what had happened. He had seen an angel. They gathered that much but he had been unable or unwilling to write more. After Elizabeth gave him some refreshment, the man who had brought him home went away and the two of them were left alone.

What happened then? Luke draws a discreet veil over what happened then. We can only surmise that it was an emotional time – many emotional times – before Zechariah had been able to communicate to Elizabeth all that had happened in the Temple and how it had devastated him. It took all her wifely love and patient understanding to work through it, but work through it they did. To Elizabeth it was good news. It was her prayer answered as she had believed it would be. She was to have a male child of her very own and he was to be the forerunner of Messiah!

Yet, she was distressed for Zechariah, her husband. What a trial for a man who was never slow to speak. But they would face it together. Elizabeth conceived and they knew a child was on the way. The angel had been right. But how would they handle it with the neighbours? They decided she would remain indoors as a natural way not to draw too much attention to themselves. They could not hide the fact that Zechariah could not speak or hear, so he was not compelled to tell everyone what had happened. They wondered if the reason for Zechariah's disability had been to keep the matter quiet until the time was right to tell it all. So he did what needed to be done out of doors and Elizabeth made her preparations for the event of her life. It was a very quiet home, compared to what they had known. For Elizabeth it was not just the joy that she was to have a child, but also that the disgrace she had suffered all these years was being taken away (v.25).

An Unexpected Visitor

In her sixth month, there was a knock on the door. When they opened it they found it was a young cousin from Nazareth. They invited her in and she came in and greeted Elizabeth. When Elizabeth heard Mary's greeting, something dramatic happened. The baby moved within her. She had seen no angel. Nor had she had any dream. Yet she knew that this was the mother-to-be of Messiah.

She was filled with the Holy Spirit and the elderly Elizabeth found herself saying in a loud voice, to this teenage girl, 'You are the most blessed of all women, and blessed is the child you will bear! Why should this great thing happen to me, that my Lord's mother comes to visit me? For as soon as I heard your greeting, the baby within me jumped with gladness. How happy she is to believe that the

Lord's message to her will come true!' (vv.39–45).

Zechariah could only stand by and see that his wife was somehow inspired without hearing a word. Then there was more. The inspiration passed from Elizabeth to the young Mary. Elizabeth's words were so important to her. Elizabeth was the first person to believe her story. It had been nothing but shame and embarrassment in Nazareth. Even Joseph, her betrothed, was slow to believe her. She broke out into a song of praise to God, that was reminiscent of how Hannah had prayed when she handed over her child Samuel into the service of the Tabernacle (1 Sam. 2:1–10). In time Elizabeth wrote it all down for Zechariah and they were both encouraged as they saw that this was the next piece in the jigsaw that had been begun for them by the angel in the Temple.

Mary stayed three months and how they talked! Elizabeth had to go over the story of Zechariah seeing the angel in the Temple and coming out speechless. Mary capped that with her story of how the same angel had come to her and told her she was to have a child without a human father. The angel had said, 'Remember your relative Elizabeth. It is said that she cannot have children, but she herself is now six months pregnant, even though she is very old. For there is nothing that God cannot do' (vv.36–37). It was this that had given her the idea that she should get away from the gossiping tongues and come down to visit them. We can imagine how Zechariah coped with all this, waiting to get every last piece written on his slate for him. The time flew past now that they were so sure about everything.

The End of her Shame

The time was coming close for Elizabeth to give birth. They arranged for Mary to go back to Nazareth. Then it was the great day and Elizabeth gave birth to a son. Her neighbours and relatives heard how wonderfully good the Lord had been to her, and they all rejoiced with her.

When the baby was a week old, they came to circumcise him, and they were going to name him Zechariah, after his father. But his mother said, 'No! His name is to be John.'

They said to her, 'But you have no relatives with that name!' Then they made signs to his father, asking him what name he would like the boy to have.

Zechariah asked for a writing tablet and wrote, 'His name is John.' How surprised they all were! As soon as he had written the name Zechariah was able to speak again, and he started praising God. The neighbours were all filled with fear, and the news about these things spread through all the hill country of

Judea. Everyone who heard of it thought about it and asked, 'What is this child going to be?' For it was plain that the Lord's power was upon him (vv.57–66).

Now it was Zechariah's time to prophesy. All that had been pent up in him for these last many months came out in praise to God. He was ecstatic. All his reluctance to believe had gone and he uttered the longest of all the prophetic songs voiced at the Nativity.

They could now see why their prayer had been so long unanswered. Their prayer was tied up in God's plan about what was to happen to Mary who was so much younger. We do not always remember that the answer to our prayers is linked to what God is doing or going to do in other people's lives. If we want all of God's will to be done, that can involve generations to come. God thinks long thoughts.

After the resurrection, Jesus said to doubting Thomas, 'Happy are those who have not seen and yet believe.' Elizabeth is an example of that steady quiet faith.

No Ageism with God

Zechariah and Elizabeth and their role in the coming of Christ into the world demonstrate that God has a purpose for his people that does not preclude their being part of it however old they are. God is never finished with us.

He has something for us to be and to do that fits the stage in life we are in. Our difficulty can be that we keep trying to be what we were in younger days. God has new things for us to engage in that require the gifts that are in the ascendant in us now; patience, wisdom, more time to pray, more time to listen, to phone, to encourage others are valuable and much needed gifts in the church and in the world today.

William Quarrier (1829–1903), the founder of Quarriers Homes in Bridge of Weir, Scotland, illustrates the pattern. Fatherless at seven, he worked for 70 hours a week putting heads on pins for a wage of only one shilling (5p) a week. He became a journeyman shoemaker at 12 and eventually owned five shops in Glasgow. He never forgot his early experience of deprivation and as a businessman started shoeblack, news and parcels brigades for street children in the city. In 1878 he founded an orphanage in a community of cottage homes in Bridge of Weir, away from the temptations of the city. At age 64, he founded a Sanatorium for people with tuberculosis, the first in Scotland. As if that were not enough, at the age 74, he founded the first Colony for Epileptics in the UK. He demonstrates that God has much still to be done after the normal age of retirement.

4

Mary

The Lord's Obedient Servant

Luke 1:26–56, Matthew 1:18–25, 2:9–23

A Tale of Two Pregnancies

The two pregnancies came together first, when the angel Gabriel appeared to a young girl, a virgin, and told her she was to have a child. Luke dates this event by reference to another woman's experience. 'In the sixth month of Elizabeth's pregnancy God sent the angel Gabriel to a town in Galilee named Nazareth. He had a message for a young woman promised in marriage to a man named Joseph, who was a descendant of King David. Her name was Mary. The angel came to her and said, 'Peace be with you! The Lord is with you and has greatly blessed you!'

Mary was deeply troubled by the angel's message, and she wondered what his words meant. The angel said to her, 'Don't be afraid, Mary; God has been gracious to you. You will become pregnant and give birth to a son, and you will name him Jesus. He will be great and will be called the Son of the Most High God. The Lord God will make him a king, as his ancestor David was, and he will be the king of the descendants of Jacob for ever; his kingdom will never end!' Mary said to the angel, 'I am a virgin. How, then, can this be?'

It is clear from the rest of the story that Mary was asking about the sheer feasibility of what the angel had said in view of the fact that she was a virgin. It was this 'how' question that he answered. 'The angel answered, 'The Holy Spirit will come on you, and God's power will rest upon you. For this reason the holy child will be called the Son of God. Remember your relative Elizabeth. It is said that she cannot have children, but she herself is now six months pregnant, even though she is very old. For there is nothing that God cannot do.' 'I am the Lord's servant,' said Mary; 'may it happen to me as you have said.' And the angel left her (Luke 1:26–38).

That was a remarkable response on Mary's part. True, every Jewish woman hoped she would have the privilege of being the mother of Messiah. None of them, however, dreamed it would be outside the normal circumstance of family life. None of them certainly imagined it would involve the social disgrace of a young woman being pregnant out of wedlock. Yet Mary, once she had been satisfied that it was within God's power to bring this about, was ready for all that it entailed. Such total submission to God was unique.

Let us accept a date towards the end of **December** as the birth date of Jesus. There is a lot of discussion about this but let us assume it for now. That means that Mary would conceive towards the end of **March,** after the angel announced what was going to happen, say, at the end of **February.** Luke says this announcement was in the sixth month of her cousin Elizabeth's pregnancy or about 3 months before John was born to her and Zechariah in their old age. That means John was born at the end of **May or the beginning of June.** With that calendar in mind, let us try to imagine what happened in between these fixed points.

Coping with Disgrace

Remember, Mary was engaged to be married to Joseph. When do you think Mary would tell Joseph about her seeing the angel and being pregnant? It would be the end of April at the earliest when she knew she was going to have a baby. We can imagine her excitement and thrill on the one hand. But she would be worried, indeed terrified, about how Joseph and others would take it. It was a terrible prospect. Joseph was a very strict, moral, upright person. That was why she was so happy to be engaged to be married to him. Now these very character traits made it nearly certain that he would have nothing to do with her when he knew she was pregnant.

From Matthew's account Joseph did not take it well at all. When Mary 'found out that she was going to have a baby by the Holy Spirit, Joseph .... did not want to disgrace Mary publicly; so he made plans to break the engagement privately' (Matt. 1:19). There was no question – he had to break the engagement with Mary, but it would be arranged as discreetly as possible. We can imagine the agony for them both in the talks they had for very different reasons. I wonder what Joseph did believe at that point.

How was it to be handled? There is no hint of her confiding in her mother. Was she an orphan? Or if her mother were alive, did she automatically take the view that everyone else in a strict Jewish community took. The age-old device was used. Mary got ready and hurried off in **April** to the hill country of Judea. That served the dual purpose of finding out if the angel had been right about Elizabeth being pregnant and taking Mary away from the glare of prying eyes in Nazareth as her pregnancy became apparent. Excuses were made and she was sent off to visit relatives, most likely escorted by some trustworthy friend. We can imagine this first journey south of about 80 miles at a walking pace, say, early in **May,** before it was obvious that she was pregnant.

Let us pause and ask who knew, at this point, what was happening. I think it might only have been Joseph and Mary and perhaps her travelling companion, and Joseph did not accept her story. It must have been an unhappy journey of 3–7 days with all the time in the world to brood.

An Unbelievable Welcome

Mary duly arrived at the home of Zacharias, who had become dumb, and Elizabeth, who was about six months ahead of her in her pregnancy. Imagine her unbelievable surprise when, 'she went into Zechariah's house and greeted Elizabeth .... and Elizabeth was filled with the Holy Spirit and said in a loud voice, "You are the most blessed of all women, and blessed is the child you will bear! Why should this great thing happen to me, that my Lord's mother comes to visit me? For as soon as I heard your greeting, the baby within me jumped with gladness. How happy is she who believes that the Lord's message to her will come true!" (Luke 1:40–45)

When she heard these words, it was unbelievable! Before Mary had said a word of explanation, Elizabeth knew! She was perhaps only the fourth person to know and was the first we read of, other than Mary herself, who believed what was happening. No wonder Mary herself burst into her own song. She was not deluded! There was at least one other person who believed her story and this was Elizabeth, her cousin, the person that the angel had mentioned. She herself was pregnant by divine intervention. It was going to be all right! She burst into poetic praise to God.

Her heart praised the Lord. Her soul was glad because of God her Saviour, He had remembered her, his lowly servant!

From now on all people would call her happy, because of the great things the Mighty God had done for her.

It was as though the words of Hannah's song she had heard from childhood became her own words (1 Sam. 2:1–10).

She was carried along by an unstoppable joy. She was to be the mother of Messiah, who would come to set right everything that was wrong in the world.

He would show mercy to those who honour him.

He would stretch out his mighty arm and scatter the proud with all their plans.

He would bring down mighty kings like Herod from their thrones, and lift up the lowly.

He would fill the hungry with good things, and send the rich away with empty hands.

He was about to keep the promise he made to their ancestors, and come to the help of his servant Israel.

He would remember to show mercy to Abraham and to all his descendants for ever! (Luke 1: 46–55)

It was all quite wonderful. Though just a lowly servant, she had honoured God and was overwhelmed that God had a commission for her.

The Waiting Time

There followed a few months staying in the welcoming and accepting home of Zechariah and Elizabeth. She could talk openly about all that had happened and what it might mean. Elizabeth also had someone she could talk to without resorting to a slate all the time. The silent homestead began to be full of talk again. Mary got the whole story of Zechariah's visit to the Temple and why he was deaf and dumb. Mary was safe and secure with only one worry. What about Joseph? But God was active in Nazareth also.

Joseph's Agony

Joseph also was worried and afraid. He could not get Mary out of his mind. 'While he was thinking about it all, an angel of the Lord appeared to him in a dream and said, "Joseph, descendant of David, do not be afraid to take

Mary to be your wife. For it is by the Holy Spirit that she has conceived. She will have a son, and you will name him Jesus – because he will save his people from their sins."

What a relief! He had his own angel and the message was the same as Mary's. She was carrying Messiah who would forgive the sins of the people. I imagine he sent word or went himself to Judea to ask her to come back. She went back to Nazareth in **June** just before the birth of John.

How was it at Nazareth then, when she arrived back about four months pregnant? We do not know but I do not think it was straightforward or easy. It was a very strict society. Years later they taunted Jesus the man about his being 'born of fornication' (John 8:41 AV).

An Unwelcome Census
The story picks up again when it was announced by the authorities that they had to go South, the 80 miles again, to Bethlehem to register in a census. They received this news with mixed emotions. They were relieved at getting away from the gossiping tongues. They were concerned about where they would be when the baby arrived for it would certainly be while they were away.

We know the story. These annoying government regulations landed them in

Bethlehem when the baby was due. There was no relative to take them in and no room in any of the inns. The baby was born in a stable in the animals' hay box. So with a six-month-old John in the hill country of Judea and a days-old baby in Bethlehem, the tale of the two pregnancies came to its fulfilment.

Confirmations Along the Way

In the loneliness of the humble birthplace, Joseph and Mary had confirmation of what was happening to them. Some shepherds came and told of a vision they had, on the hillside, of an angel, who told them to come and see the baby that was born to save their people.

Other confirmations came six weeks later when they went up the six miles to present Jesus in the temple in Jerusalem. They found a man, Simeon, and a woman, Anna, who also had been told by God that Jesus was Messiah. The final corroboration came from some astrologers. They arrived saying that their reading of the stars brought them to the conclusion that a child had been born who would be King of the Jews. They had made a 1,000 mile journey to come and offer gifts to the new-born king.

That was the end of the good news for them. Trouble followed. The astrologers had created a scare in the palace in Jerusalem and soon soldiers were swarming everywhere looking for the child to kill him. They had warning of this

and before the massacre of the infants they got
out as refugees by travelling the 200 mile journey
to Egypt. They not only had all the stress of
being strangers in a foreign country, they had
to keep quiet about why they were there. They
could not tell their story for security reasons
(Matt. 2:13).

We do not know how long they were in
Egypt. Two years is the traditional time. When
they came back, they considered settling in Judea
but were warned in a dream not to do so – again
for security reasons. So they went back to
Nazareth (Matt. 2:22-23).

The Thoughtful Mother

It is hard to believe that what Mary
experienced from the time she saw the angel
until they were back in Nazareth after Egypt,
took place in the years that we would call her
late teens. What a vote of confidence this is in
young people as God sees them. We are never
too young to begin to be obedient to God and
start to fulfil his purposes for us.

We need to note, however, that the most
frequently mentioned response of Mary was
thoughtfulness. When the angel Gabriel
appeared to her in Nazareth, 'She was deeply
troubled and wondered what his words meant'
(Luke 1:29). Only after she was assured about
the 'how' of the angel's message, did she accept
the role that was offered to her.

After the shepherds had gone back to their sheep, 'Mary remembered all these things and thought deeply about them' (Luke 2:19). After the incident in the Temple when Jesus was 12 years old, 'His mother treasured all these thing in her heart' (Luke 2:51). Mary did not rush at things. She considered them and when she was satisfied in her mind, her response was obedience equally to the voice of God and to the requirements of his Law. It is not surprising then that the last word we hear from her about Jesus, was at the wedding in Cana of Galilee, 'Do whatever he says!' (John 2:5)

5

Joseph

The God-Appointed Guardian

Matthew 1:18–25, 2:9–23; Luke 2:1–40

Joseph was a respected carpenter in the town of Nazareth toward the end of the reign of Herod The Great. He was of a good family. He had a reputation for being both strict in his morals, and sensitive to others. He had royal blood in his veins. Oddly, although an indispensable player in the divine drama, he is not recorded as having spoken one word during any of the incidents in which he took part. We have to imagine his story from the circumstantial evidence.

A Dream becomes a Nightmare
He hoped to make a good marriage to a young woman, also of royal blood. Her name was Mary. Like any responsible young man, he dreamed of all that they would be to each other and to the community when the time came

for them to be married.

One day in the spring, when his spirits were bright and his heart was full, Mary asked to speak with him about a very personal matter. She told him that she was pregnant but he was not to jump to conclusions. She tried to say that an angel had appeared to her and told her that God's power would rest on her and she would become pregnant and give birth to a son who would be the Son of God. On the face of it, it was a ridiculous story, and his faith in Mary was strained to the limit. How much of Mary's story he really heard through his pain, we do not know. We only know that he was devastated and felt he could not go on with the marriage. How could a person of principle, as he tried to be, go on with an arrangement where there was going to be a child conceived out of wedlock, when he was not even the father? His dream of a happy marriage had become a nightmare.

He still cared for Mary and decided he would not do anything rash or publicly shame her. Mary made this a little easier by suggesting that she go to visit a cousin, Elizabeth, and her priest husband Zechariah about 80 miles south in the hill country of Judea. Apparently, the angel that had appeared to her, had mentioned something about old Elizabeth having a baby too. So she got ready and went off with a travelling companion on the journey

south. It took a week or more and she stayed
for about three months.

Joseph was left with his shattered dream
and the problem of what to do when she came
back and was evidently carrying a child. It was
a nightmare, even to think about it, as he tried
to forget about it by applying himself to his
work at his carpenter's bench. The place was
empty without Mary and his thoughts were
never far away from her. Then Joseph had a
real dream.

Dream One

'While he was thinking about this, an angel of
the Lord appeared to him in a dream and said,
"Joseph, descendant of David, do not be afraid
to take Mary to be your wife. For it is by the
Holy Spirit that she has conceived. She will
have a son, and you will name him Jesus –
because he will save his people from their sins."
Matthew the writer of the gospel comments
that all this happened in order to make what
the Lord had said through the prophet come
true, 'A virgin will become pregnant and have
a son and he will be called Immanuel, (which
means) 'God is with us' (Matt. 1:20–23).

Mary's angel was now matched by one that
appeared to him in his own dream. The
message was the same. His heart was
wonderfully relieved. His dream of marriage
had not died. It was going to be more

wonderful than ever. They were to bring up Messiah. He was to be Messiah's guardian.

I imagine he shut up shop and set off to go to Judea to bring Mary back. When she got back, she was seen to be about four months pregnant. Joseph, however, was unashamed and they went ahead and got married. Out of respect for Mary and in the light of their angelic visitations, they decided not to consummate the marriage until after the child was born. Before that could happen, however, the state interfered. The Roman Emperor, Caesar Augustus, decreed that there was to be a census of all the people in the New Roman Empire. It was to provide the foundation on which the administration would be based and the people would be taxed. The decree also said that every one had 'to register himself, each to his own town'. So, they had to get on the road a second time and go south from Nazareth to Judea. This time, it was not to the home of Zechariah and Elizabeth, but to the town of Bethlehem in Judea, the birthplace of King David. Joseph went there because he was a descendant of David (Matt. 1:1–17).

This was not a pleasant journey for Mary who was almost at term for the birth of her child. Whether they both walked or perhaps Joseph was able to afford a donkey for Mary, as tradition imagines, the road was rough and the weather cold. Joseph's thoughts were full of foreboding as he watched his wife struggling along.

They arrived safely and in the nick of time. Joseph hunted for lodgings, but they were all taken by the other people who had come to register in the census. As a last resort, he found an innkeeper who allowed them to bed down in the place where the animals were tethered. 'While they were in Bethlehem, the time came for her to have her baby.' With Joseph looking on and acting as midwife, 'Mary gave birth to her first son, wrapped him in strips of cloth and laid him in a manger' (Luke 2:7). Up until that point it had been a very ordinary event which Joseph was relieved had gone off so well. They had the normal inexpressible joy of seeing their new-born baby.

Visitors in the Night
Joseph and Mary had some privacy, being together with only the animals and the baby. Then, the same night, totally unexpectedly, the place was visited by some very excited shepherds telling the couple a most remarkable story. They had, as usual, been spending the night in the fields, taking care of their flocks. All of a sudden, an angel of the Lord appeared to them, and the glory of the Lord shone over them. They were terribly afraid, but the angel told them not to be afraid! He said he was there with good news for them and not only for

them but for everybody. That very day, they
were told, their Saviour had been born in
Bethlehem, the town that King David had
come from. He was both their Messiah and
their Lord! As a sign that this was true they
were told to go to Bethlehem and they would
find a baby wrapped in strips of cloth but,
unusually, lying in a manger. There was more
about a choir of angels, and they set off
immediately to find out if it was true.

They did not need to ask. There in front of
their eyes, were Mary and Joseph, and the baby
lying in the manger. When the shepherds saw
him, they told the couple what the angel had
said about him. By this time a crowd had
gathered and everyone who heard it were
amazed at what the shepherds said. When the
shepherds and the crowd had gone, Joseph saw
that Mary was very quiet about it all. She
needed time to take it all in and wonder what
it was going to mean in the future.

The Naming Ceremony
A week later, the baby, as a good Jew, was
circumcised. Joseph and Mary had no
difficulty about a name. Each had been told
by their angel that it was to be Jesus and Jesus
it was, a name full of strange promise that they
could not imagine at the time (Luke 2:21).
Around this time they found accommodation
in Bethlehem.

Dedication in the Temple

A little more than a month later, Joseph and Mary travelled the six miles from Bethlehem to the Temple in Jerusalem for the customary ceremony of dedication. They took Jesus to present him to the Lord, in the Temple with a sacrifice. They could only afford the lesser offering of two young pigeons. It was a symbolic way of recognizing that Jesus, their baby, belonged to God. They did not know it but they were in for another big surprise.

At that time there was an old man named Simeon living in Jerusalem. He was a good, God-fearing man. The Holy Spirit was with him and had assured him that he would not die before he had seen the Lord's promised Messiah. Led by the Spirit, Simeon went into the Temple. When the parents brought the child Jesus into the Temple, Simeon took the child in his arms and gave thanks to God. Then he prophesied that the baby would be a light to all the people of the world. Joseph and Mary were amazed at this. Then he blessed them both and turned to Mary and warned her that Jesus would be a very controversial figure and this would be heart-breaking for her.

To crown that day for Joseph and Mary in the Temple, Anna, an elderly, devout widow also noticed the baby and publicly gave thanks for the child and spoke about him to everyone she knew who was also waiting for God's promises for Jerusalem to be fulfilled (Luke 2:22–38).

Dream Two

Back in Bethlehem the final event of their stay there proved to be both awesome and troubling. A small caravan of important-looking men made their way to their door. They were astrologers who had been directed to Bethlehem by Herod the Great. They wanted to come into the house to see the child, because they said they had seen his star in the East and believed he was born to be king. They not only came in, they brought expensive gifts of gold and frankincense and myrrh for him. They kneeled before him and worshipped him. They did not stay long.

That night after they were gone, Joseph had a second dream. 'An angel of the Lord again appeared in a dream to Joseph and said, "Herod will be looking for the child in order to kill him. So get up, take the child and his mother and escape to Egypt, and stay there until I tell you to leave." Joseph got up, took the child and his mother, and left during the night for Egypt, where they stayed as refugees until Herod died.'

Dream Three

After Herod died, an angel of the Lord appeared in a third dream to Joseph in Egypt and said, 'Get up, take the child and his mother, and go back to the land of Israel, because those who tried to kill the child are dead.' So Joseph got up, took the child and his mother, and went back to Israel (Matt. 2:19–21).

Dream Four

But when Joseph heard that Archelaus had succeeded his father Herod as King of Judea, he was afraid to go there. He was given instructions in a fourth dream, so he went to the province of Galilee and made his home in a town named Nazareth (Matt. 2:22–23). There things settled down and they got on with the ordinary business of raising a family and earning a living by carpentry. There were more children, four brothers and at least two sisters (Mark 6:3). Jesus grew and became strong; he was full of wisdom and God's blessing was on him.

The Guardian

Joseph's God-given and God-guided task was to guard the child Jesus and his mother, Mary. He provided security by becoming the legal husband of Mary and father of Jesus. He protected her from the shame that might otherwise have dogged her because of the circumstances of Jesus' birth. His genealogy made it necessary for the couple to be in

Bethlehem for the census. He aided in bringing to pass the prophecy of Micah about Messiah being born in Bethlehem.

When danger threatened, God used a dream to warn them of the danger from Herod. His prompt action got Jesus away from the murdering soldiers just in time. This same gift of dreams was used to get the little family back from Egypt and north to Nazareth in Galilee.

There Joseph resumed his trade of carpentry and was the bread winner and the human father to the growing boy. His contribution to the physical outworking of the incarnation was indispensable, yet he never said a word that was recorded. He is a very strong reminder of the fact that God has a need of people just to care for and take care of others if their work for God is to be done.

6

Augustus

The Right Time

'But when the right time finally came,
God sent his own Son. He came as the
son of a human mother and lived under
the Jewish Law' (Gal.4:4). 'It came to pass
in those days, that there went out a decree
from Caesar Augustus, that all the world
should be taxed' (Luke 2:1 AV).

A Peacemaker
'Those days' were about halfway through the
41-year reign of Caesar Augustus, the founder
and the first ruler of the Roman Empire. They
were remarkable days. They were days of
peace. Before Augustus became the sole ruler,
civil war had torn the Roman Republic apart
for half a century, and dragged many of
Rome's subject peoples into the death-dealing
conflict.

The last gasp of those struggles had been
the war between Octavian (later to be called
Augustus) and Antony and Cleopatra. It

ranged over Egypt and the Middle East. After their armies and their fleet had been defeated, both committed suicide. Anthony fell on his sword and Cleopatra died from a snake bite from an asp that she had smuggled into her bedroom in a basket of figs in 27BC. Shakespeare immortalized the scenes at the end of his play *Antony and Cleopatra*.

That was about 20 years before the birth of Jesus. They had been 20 years of peace. The people had become weary of war and so had their new ruler. They were particularly weary of civil war where brother fought against brother and friend against friend in a struggle for which they had little heart. Homesteads were destroyed and they were seldom able to plant and harvest their crops without molestation.

Peace was what they valued most of the benefits brought to them by Caesar Augustus. 'Everyone found the sweet taste of peace seductive,' said Tacitus their historian. Augustus built fleets, suppressed piracy and made the Mediterranean Sea safe for trading vessels. He limited foreign wars by deciding not to expand Rome any further. He was content with the natural boundaries: the Atlantic Ocean on the West, the Rhine and the Danube on the North, the Euphrates in the East and towards the South, the sandy deserts of Arabia and Africa. Significantly, there is no reference in the New Testament to war or current conflict. The 'Pax Romana' was real. But there was more.

A Dispenser of Justice

'A decree went out.' Caesar Augustus created a whole new kind of state. The history of the period sounds amazingly contemporary. He restored the rule of law and constitutional government. Vigour returned to the laws, authority to the courts, prestige to the Senate and the powers of the magistrates were renewed. He established a police force. Justice could be obtained. The machinery of bringing complaints to Rome was greatly improved as Paul the Apostle found out when a mere appeal to Caesar brought him from Jerusalem to Rome to be tried (Acts 25:11).

Augustus turned the armies of different generals into one long-service professional army. He paid his soldiers regularly and well and saw to it that they received a liberal gratuity when they were discharged. He was able to demobilize 300,000 veteran soldiers from his army and settled them, each on their own piece of land, as peasant farmers in Italy and in other parts of the empire. Sometimes he bought this land out of his own funds when the funds of the state were inadequate. Some of these veterans became benefactors of the local community like the centurion of whom the people of Capernaum spoke so highly (Luke 7:1–10).

The principle of payment for public service from the public purse was accepted and it seems that all the public servants may have received salaries except the magistrates. In fact, it was the beginning of a Civil Service.

'That all the world should be taxed.' He initiated censuses to create a reasonable and fair tax system. He set himself to acquire exact knowledge of the resources of the Empire and attempted to equalize the burden of taxation, which was a very difficult task. It was one of his censuses that brought Joseph and the pregnant Mary to Bethlehem where Jesus was born (Luke 2:1–3).

Augustus made every effort to ensure that wealth should be equitably distributed and the revenues of the state should be collected honestly and expended in such a way that the subjects of Rome might regard her rule as a blessing and not a curse. Matthew and Zacchaeus were later appointees of this system.

He drew up annual financial statements of the resources of the state and at his death left a summary account of the whole empire. He introduced property taxes in Italy. He levied death duties and a tax on the sale of goods by auction and other taxes on the purchase and release of slaves. He even reduced taxes or remitted them where he could.

A Stimulus to Development

He initiated measures to develop the infrastructure in ways that sounds very modern. He ordered his commanders to use their soldiers to construct roads and build bridges in the area where they were stationed and pay for it out of their booty. These Roman roads became proverbial and made communication easy throughout the empire.

He required wealthy citizens to build great buildings in Rome and other cities and he himself set the example. It is said that he found Rome a city of brick and left it a city of marble. He paved the streets of Rome; he ensured its water supply by building great aqueducts; he created drainage systems. He provided public baths and restored fountains that had been long neglected by the government of the Senate before the civil wars. In all these ways he provided employment for the people.

He built huge granaries and kept a steady supply of grain coming in to fill them. Food was distributed by streets. Public games were created for the entertainment of the people. He reduced the proportion of the poor in Rome by ten per cent even when the population was increasing.

Nor did he neglect religion. He returned statues stolen from temples and got rid of 80 statues of himself and made them into golden tripods as offerings in the temple of Apollo.

He caused temples to be built and encouraged people to honour the gods.

During the reign of Augustus, beyond doubt, a new page was turned in the history of humankind. It was in no small measure due to the fact that his administration lasted for 41 years. He established himself 20 years before the birth of Jesus and went on to rule for another 20 years while Jesus was growing up. His was the longest rule of any of the Roman Emperors. The average tenure of the office of Emperor for the next 500 years was only eight years. Twenty of the Emperors reigned for only a year or less. Augustus achieved as much as he did because he was in power so long. To see how much the stability of a government is needed for consolidating achievements, we only need to compare the progress and creativity that was enjoyed in England under the 45-year reign of Elizabeth I (1558–1603) and the 64-year reign over Britain of Queen Victoria (1837–1901).

A Master of Spin

Augustus has been called, 'the master of spin' (BBC Radio 4, May 1999). He was a master at presenting what he did in the way he wanted it to be regarded. He left a document detailing the achievements of his administration. It is called *Res Gestae* or 'What I Accomplished', and he had parts of it engraved on bronze pillars in a public place. The original document no longer exists but there are enough quotations of it in other works to let us know its contents. It is true that we often get Augustus' gloss on his achievements, but that takes nothing away from their number and extent.

He was the first to have coins with his head embossed on them mass manufactured in Gaul and used as currency throughout the Empire. 'Whose image is this?' asked Jesus and it was Caesar's. So he achieved what today we would call high logo and name recognition.

He deliberately maintained a modest style. When he returned victorious to Rome he surrendered all his power to the Senate and the Assembly of the people and only took back functions when they agreed he should have them. He made sure that any action he took had the sanction of the Senate. When it came to titles, he refused any title that would have signified that he was the king or any kind of sole ruler. He accepted 'Augustus' which means someone who is revered for good cause.

He patronized the arts. 'The Augustan Age of Literature' was one of the most famous and productive in the history of letters. The poet Virgil wrote his epic poem *The Aeneid* to tell the story of Rome from ancient times, culminating in Augustus.

This, this is he whom thou so oft hearest
promised to thee, Augustus Caesar, son
of a god, who shall again set up the golden
age.....' (Virgil *Aeneid* VI:791–3)

'Now is come the last age ....
The great line of the centuries begins
anew.
Now the Virgin returns, the reign of
Saturn returns;
now a new generation descends from
heaven on high.
Only do thou ...smile on the birth of the
child under whom the iron brood shall
cease,
and a golden race spring up throughout
the world. (Virgil *Eclogues* IV:4–10)

Some Christians, because it spoke about the
coming birth of a divine child , saw it as a
pagan foreshadowing of the coming of Jesus.
This view was even made official by the
Emperor Constantine in 330AD.

We still read the works of other famous
names in literature from the Augustan Age,
like the poets, Horace and Ovid, the historian
Livy, and others. All of these undoubtedly
became part of the Public Relations output of
Augustus and used language that today we
would call utopian. They expressed the hopes
and aspirations that people always have, that

seemed, under Augustus, to be coming closer to fulfilment than they had ever dreamed possible.

This hope was not just local to Rome or to Italy. ' .. that all the world should be taxed.' It was found throughout 'the whole Roman world', as the later versions more accurately translate it (Luke 2:1).

A World Empire

Luke implies that the backdrop to the cradle where Jesus was born was the founding of the Roman Empire by Caesar Augustus. 'Everyone, then, went to register himself, each to his own town. Joseph went from the town of Nazareth in Galilee to the town of Bethlehem in Judea, the birthplace of King David. Joseph went there because he was a descendant of David. He went to register with Mary, who was promised in marriage to him. She was pregnant'.

What could have remained a puny local event came to be of world significance because of the context in which it occurred. The womb out of which the universal Kingdom of God would be born, was the greatest secular empire that the world had known up until that time.

A New Concept

The concept of 'the Gospel', or 'The Evangel' that Jesus and his followers used, was coloured, if not formed, by the language used to describe the difference that Augustus made to the world of that day. In 9BC the proconsul of Asia wrote an inscription marking the birthday of Augustus (23 September) which gives us the feel of this utopian thinking. It reads,

> It is a day which we may justly count as the beginning of everything, in the benefit it brings.
>
> It has restored the shape of everything that was failing and turning into misfortune, and has given a new look to the Universe at the time when it would gladly have welcomed destruction if Caesar had not been born to be the common blessing of all men ....
>
> The Providence which has ordered the whole of our life, has ordained the most perfect consummation for human life by giving to it Augustus, by filling him with virtue for doing the work of a benefactor among men, and by sending in him, as it were, a saviour for us and those who come after us, to make war to cease, to create order everywhere. ....
>
> The birthday of the god Augustus was the beginning for the world of **glad tidings (EVANGEL)** that have come to us through him.' (From *Alexander to Constantine* by E. Barker p. 211f)

This throws light on the pronouncement of the Angels to the shepherds. 'Behold I bring you **glad tidings (EVANGEL)** of great joy which shall be to all people. .....Glory to God and on earth peace, good will toward men.'

It is significant that the birth of Jesus and the proclamation of the angels came right in the middle of the reign of Augustus, when the hopes of many peoples were probably at their highest. Tiberius Caesar came to power in 14AD and everything began to go downhill again. It continued to go down through Caligula, Claudius and Nero and most of those who followed. The public ministry of Jesus, as Luke tells us, began only after the decline of Rome began to set in under Tiberius and his henchman Sejanus (Luke 3:1).

The head of Tiberius was on the coin that Jesus looked at and asked, 'Whose image is this?' When he was told, 'Caesar's!' he declared, 'Render to Caesar the things that are Caesar's and to God the things that are God's!'

Competing Kingdoms

This is why Luke registered that the birth of Jesus was in 'those days when a decree went out from Caesar Augustus, that all the world should be taxed.' It was as though the historian, Luke, is saying, 'there is an alternative way to go for people to find their aspirations fulfilled. There is an alternative leader to Caesar Augustus. However good he has been or will be, it can only be for a time and his successors will be flawed and disappointed in the end.'

Luke was affirming that God rules in the affairs of men by his dating of the birth of Jesus and the beginning of his ministry by reference to Augustus and Tiberias Caesar. Jesus God's son is the Lord of History.

He was calling for a choice in real historical time, symbolized by the manger in Bethlehem and the Court of Caesar in Rome. Much later, the Jewish leaders, said to Pilate, the Roman Governor, when they were persuading him to execute Jesus, 'If you let this man go, you are not Caesar's friend.'

Today the good news of Christ has spread through all the world to an extent not even conceivable when Jesus was born, yet foreseen by him (Matt. 24:14). God knows the names and works and ends of every ruler in the world today. The gospels tell us this to encourage us when evil and chaos seem to triumph. The last word will be with him who was born to be king in the reign of Caesar Augustus.

7

The Shepherds

The Hills were Alive

Luke 2:8–20

The next vehicles for the revelation of this new event, the birth of Messiah, were some shepherds in that part of the country who were spending the night in the fields, taking care of their flocks (Luke 2:8). Their significance is that they brought to Joseph and Mary the independent corroboration that Mary's son was the Saviour, the Messiah and the Son of God. Since the angel-appearances to Zechariah, Mary and Joseph there had been no word from heaven that we know about for some months. Many things had been difficult for Joseph and Mary. The hostility of their community, the long and arduous journey south to register in Bethlehem, their failure to get decent lodgings, and, finally, her giving birth to a son in a stable outside a place that was crowded with people, none of whom they knew.

For the shepherds to arrive with their account of the appearance of the angels to them in the night of the birth of the child, must have been a unique kind of corroboration of all that they had heard and believed up to that point. We learn little from the text about the shepherds.

The Poverty of their Station

Earlier in the history of the Jews, shepherds provided the picture that best described what a good ruler should be. David was the shepherd king, who spoke of God being his shepherd. (Psalm 23:1) All the prophets criticized the leaders in Israel because they neglected and took advantage of the people, their God-given flock. Messiah was to be an exemplary shepherd (Eze. 34:1–10).

In recent times, however, we know from other sources that shepherds were poor and despised. 'No position in the world, is as despised as that of the shepherd' (Midrash on Psalm 23). This contempt for shepherds was not only economic, because they were poor. It was religious. On account of their work they were often unable to keep the details of the ceremonial law. They could not observe all the meticulous hand washings and rules and regulations. Their flocks made far too constant demands on them and strict Jews looked down on them.

It would have made this hypocrisy worse if these shepherds were the same as those who supplied the sheep and lambs for the daily sacrifices in the Temple, only a few miles away. We know that the Temple flocks were pastured near Bethlehem. If they were the Temple shepherds, they had to be expert in their work. The animals for the sacrifices had to be without blemish, if they were to be acceptable to God. It would be ironic if these shepherds who looked after the Temple lambs were the first to see the Lamb of God who takes away the sin of the world.

The poverty of the shepherds is in keeping with the picture of poverty in which Mary brought Jesus into the world. His cot was a manger. They could only afford a pauper's sacrifice of two pigeons when they went to dedicate him in the Temple. Even in his birth, the human vessels through which the revelation of his divine origin was confirmed were among the poor and despised of the world.

The Celebration in their Vision
When a Jewish boy was born, it was an occasion of great joy and rejoicing in which friends, relatives and neighbours joined. Jesus was born in a stable in Bethlehem. Mary and Joseph were far from their friends and neighbours, so they were cut off from that

communal joy. But there was a celebration of a totally unexpected kind. It happened in several stages.

Some shepherds were carrying out their normal nightly duties of watching their sheep out in the hills to protect them from thieves and beasts of prey. It was not the easiest part of their day, especially if the weather was cold and wet. They may have had a fire to keep them warm and warn off the predators. They became aware of the light from the fire increasing unaccountably. As it became brighter and brighter they became conscious of an angel from the Lord approaching them. The incandescent light was the glory of the Lord and it enveloped them. They were terrified and showed it. Then the angel spoke, 'There is no need to be afraid. I am the bearer of good news. It is good news for you, but for more than you. It will be good news for everybody. This very day over there in Bethlehem, David's town, your Saviour was born. He is Messiah your Lord!'

It would seem that they were not very sure about this. It had come unexpectedly and was a unique experience for these very ordinary men. The angel continued, 'This is what will prove it to you: you will find a baby wrapped in strips of cloth and lying in a manger.' There was to be a physical event that would corroborate this powerful numinous experience they were having.

Before they could react to that, the experience moved into its second stage. The light became even brighter and a great army of heaven's angels joined their solitary angel, singing praises to God. In a resounding chorus they sang, 'Glory to God in the highest heaven, and peace on earth to those with whom he is pleased!' We do not know how many times they sang their chorus, but eventually they withdrew and night again enveloped the shepherds.

The third stage shows how impressive and convincing they must have found the experience. They agreed to go to Bethlehem to see the thing that had happened that the Lord himself had told them. There is just a hint that this was a considerable distance, but they were determined to go as quickly as they could and they went.

It appears that with little difficulty they found the place. In the fourth stage of that exciting night, they found Mary and Joseph and saw the baby lying in the manger. Since this corroborated what the angel had said, they recited their experience to the total amazement of the young couple and some others who had been attracted to the place. These happenings gave Mary even more to think about and, over time, she thought deeply about them. They had no friends and neighbours to celebrate with them their joy in the birth of Jesus. They had an even more wonderful celebration where heaven and earth joined in giving thanks to God. Whether it was still night or in the early dawn, the shepherds went back singing praises to God.

The Clarity of their Revelation

There were not many words spoken that night by the angel, yet their significance cannot be denied. 'This very day over there in Bethlehem, David's town, your Saviour was born. He is Messiah your Lord!' They were told three things. The child who had been born was their 'Saviour'. They knew that word. It was often on their lips when they prayed and asked God to get them out of some difficulty. They knew that God had often saved them from dangers and disasters. It had another meaning and the next thing that the angel said meant that he was using it with its other meaning.

This Saviour that had been born was also Messiah. They knew that word too. Their country was under Roman rule. Before that they had been under other foreign rulers. They had not had a real king of their own for about 500 years. Their prophets had told them why. They had forgotten God and broken his law. The prophets had also told them that one day he would 'anoint' another man to be their

King and he would be like David their best king. Messiah they called him, for it just means the anointed person in Hebrew. In Greek the word is 'Christ'. Messiah would save them from their enemies (Luke 1:69–70). He would liberate them from the Romans. It was their great hope and they prayed for Messiah to come and women prayed that he would be their child.

The third thing the angel told the shepherds was that he would be their 'Lord'. That was puzzling because this word also had two possible meanings. It was what the Roman Emperor was called. Messiah would be an alternative ruler. That made sense if he was to save them from the Romans. The other meaning was more strange. Jews felt the name of God was so holy that they should not even say it. They made up another word that they felt they could say. It was translated into Greek as 'Lord'. With this meaning the angels would be saying that Messiah was divine. This was a surprise.

It was only a few words and they were relatively simple words for uneducated men. But their significance was enormous. They needed to be checked out. The angel had recognized this and had told them how they could prove it. If they went over to Bethlehem, they would find a baby just born that day. He would not be in a normal home. He would be

lying in a manger among cattle. They went
without delay to explore and they found the
place and 'It had been just as the angel had
told them.' They had their proof and Mary
and Joseph had corroboration of their previous
revelations.

The Spontaneity of their Response

With anything miraculous, there is always
what God does and what is left to people to
do. God sent the angel and gave them a unique
experience of an angelic appearance. They
acted on what the angel had said and went in
search of the child. They wanted to know.
They put it to the test. They found it to be
true. In uninhibited fashion they told their
experience to the couple and some others who
had gathered round. Then they went back to
their humdrum lives as shepherds but with a
song in their hearts and a spring in their step.

All through this book we must have
noticed the rough simplicity of the birth of
the Son of God. We might have expected that,
if he had to be born into this world at all, it
would be in a palace or a mansion. There was
a European monarch who worried his court
by often disappearing and walking incognito
amongst his people. When he was asked not
to do so for security's sake, he answered. 'I
cannot rule my people unless I know how they
live.' It is the great truth of the Christian faith

that we have a God who knows the life we live because he too lived it and claimed no special advantage over ordinary people.

Luke heard the shepherds' story, probably from Mary, and wrote it down for us. There were several lessons in it. God speaks simply to ordinary people and they can understand what he says, check it out for themselves and have their whole outlook changed. When God speaks, there is a corporate side to it. It has significance not just for the recipient individuals but for others with whom they are in touch. God does not speak like this every day. There are special times but most times are routine and ordinary. When God speaks to us, we ought to be ready to share it with others.

8

Simeon

Ready to Die

Luke 2: 22–35

A Very Jewish Jew

We are back at Herod's Temple. Jesus had a
very Jewish start to his life. He was
circumcised on time, on the eighth day. He
was given a very Jewish name Jesus (=Joshua
= saviour). This was the first public use of the
name that they had both independently been
given by an angel (Luke 2:21). Thirty-two days
later, Joseph and young Mary made the six
mile journey to Jerusalem and the Temple to
conform to the rites for their first-born son.
It meant presenting him to the priest in the
Temple with an offering of a lamb and a
pigeon, or two pigeons, if that was all the
family could afford. Joseph and young Mary
were so poor that they were only able to afford
the two pigeons (Lev. 12:6–8). The ceremony
underlined the fact that the child belonged to

God and was given back to them on trust. It
was an awe-inspiring event for them in the
august setting of Herod's Temple at the top
of Temple Mount. Suddenly, an old man
stepped forward and asked to take the child in
his arms.

Delayed Death

This was 'a man named Simeon'. He lived in
Jerusalem and was a good and God-fearing
man. He was one of the people who were
waiting with expectancy for Messiah to come
and save Israel. But Simeon was different. He
was a man controlled by the Holy Spirit and
the Spirit had actually told him that he would
not die before he had seen God's Messiah. We
would all like to know how the Spirit revealed
this to him and there has been speculation
about it.

One legend has it that he was engaged in
the translation of the Old Testament into
Greek. One day it was his turn to render some
of the prophet Isaiah from Hebrew into
Greek. All went well for the first six chapters.
But when they came to the seventh chapter,
and to the verse in that chapter, 'Behold, a
virgin shall conceive, and bear a son, and shall
call his name Immanuel,' Simeon threw down
his pen at that impossible prophecy and would
write no more. 'How can this be?' he asked.
And in spite of the arguments of the others

Simeon would not subscribe his name to the 'virgin' passage that seemed to satisfy and delight the rest. In anger he threw down his pen and went home to his own house.

But at midnight an angel appeared to Simeon, and said to him: 'Simeon, I am Gabriel that stands in the presence of God. And, behold, you will remain alive until you see with your own eyes the LORD's Christ, made of a woman, and until the virgin's son shall put his little hand into thine aged bosom, and shall there loose the silver cord of your life.' And it was so.

This is only a legend but something happened, perhaps just a growing conviction, that restrained him from dying until he had seen Messiah. Pastors quite often see this tendency in people with terminal illness to fight off death until something is dealt with and then quite peacefully pass away.

A Far-Seeing Prayer

In old Simeon's case, led by the Spirit, he went into the Temple. When the parents brought the child Jesus into the Temple to dedicate him to God, Simeon took the child in his arms and gave thanks to God that he had kept his promise. He prayed to die peacefully. He was content that with his own eyes he had seen in the baby he had in his arms, God's salvation.

Then his prayer took a new turn. He said

that the salvation he was talking about had been prepared in the presence of all peoples. What had begun as a very Jewish ceremony was reaching across boundaries to encompass every nation. Simeon was digging deep into his lifetime memory of the Psalms and the prophet Isaiah and pulling out what hardly any of his contemporaries had noticed. This salvation was not just for Jews. It was to be, as Isaiah had prophesied, a light to reveal God's will to the Gentiles, the non-Jews whom Jews generally despised and looked down upon (Isa. 42:6). Of course, it would also bring glory to the people of Israel, but part of that glory would be the universal reach of this salvation.

This is a note that had not yet been struck in the songs of old Elizabeth and young Mary, or in the prophecy of Zechariah when his ears were unstopped and his lips were unsealed. The infant Jesus that Simeon held in his arms was to be the Saviour of the world, not just the Jews! No wonder Joseph and His mother marvelled at those things which were spoken about their child (Luke 2:25–33).

What did Simeon mean when he spoke about seeing God's salvation? Salvation in his day, as in ours, had as many meanings as there were people who thought about it. It had a very political meaning to those who chafed under the Roman yoke and longed for their country to be liberated from the oppressor. It had a very personal meaning to those who were struggling with financial or family circumstances with which they were not coping. It could have a very spiritual or religious meaning to people who were feeling great guilt because of their sin and failure.

We are not told what Simeon meant, just that he was very thankful for it. Whatever he meant, we know what salvation would mean if we ourselves were using the word. The wonder of the Christian gospel is that when we ask what we must do to be saved, it covers many of these things and more, whoever we are and however long we have waited.

A universally available salvation was the revelation that Simeon underlined and brought to the attention of Joseph and Mary and the bystanders that watched and heard him speak. But there was more.

The Downside

In returning the child to Mary and Joseph, Simeon blessed them too. As he did so, he struck another new note about Messiah who was there as a child. He continued in more sombre prophetic tones, especially to Mary. He told her that the child was set on a course that would bring down some people and lift up others (Luke 2:34–35). It is a picture, found in several places in the Bible, of a stone which could be a stepping-stone by which people could step up; or it could be a stumbling-block over which people tripped and fell down. It would depend on their reaction to him. It still does. We need to ask whether Mary's son has been a stumbling stone to us or the means of us rising to heights that we had not dreamed of.

Jesus would always present a challenge to those who saw or heard him. He would receive hostile criticism and even be slandered. However, even when this happened it would reveal more about his critics than about himself. There is a story of an art gallery in Italy. Two young people stood and criticized some of the paintings. They tried to involve the curator in their discussion but he replied, 'These pictures are the judge of their viewers and not the other way round.' People would reveal their secret thoughts when they engaged in speaking against him.

This was not good news for Mary, and Simeon knew it. With great tenderness he told her, 'Sorrow, like a sharp sword, will break your own heart.' And for the first, but not the last time in the nativity story, a cloud cast its shadow over the young family. At the very end, Jesus himself was still trying to get across to his disciples that the Son of Man must suffer and those who follow him cannot avoid their own cross (Luke 24:26). Trying experiences are not an optional extra to the follower of

Jesus. They are the life. The cross is never far away.

Nunc Dimittis

These Latin words are the first two words in the Latin translation of Simeon's sentiments when he took the child in his arms. They have been set to music in hundreds of versions and the song of Simeon has been sung at evensong in Catholic, Orthodox and Anglican churches all over the world every Sunday evening since at least the fourth century. I have often wondered what people think or feel as they sing these words so frequently. Do they just remember Simeon and this event in the Temple long ago? Or does it come from precarious times in the past when the likelihood of death from sickness, violence, natural disaster or other cause, was a greater possibility than today? Is it a harmonious, liturgical version of the child's evening prayer:

This night as I lie down to sleep,
I pray thee Lord my soul to keep.
If I should die before I wake,
Take me to heaven for Jesus' sake.

Certainly, if we have a full understanding of what Simeon was saying in the Temple, and the salvation that he spoke of is real in our experience, it takes the sting and terror out of death for us, even as it did for him.

Death has become almost a taboo subject today. We are living much longer and death is not so near. I have met people in their forties who were attending their first funeral. We tend to sanitize death and relegate it to the hospital or the mortuary. The Hippocratic Oath seems to drive doctors to prolong life to an inordinate length as though death was the worst thing that could happen to anyone. With supreme irony, political capital is made out of death, and funeral scenes invade our TV screens with great regularity whether it be from Northern Ireland or the Middle East or after a notorious crime.

Simeon did not have that view. He wanted to live until something happened that was important not just to him but to the world. Death had no terrors for him and it need not have for us. Indeed, to the Christian death is the best thing that will ever have happened to them. It is a gateway to a fuller life beyond the grave.

A Bible translator in the Congo illustrated this. He was talking with a Congolese man whose father-in-law had died. According to African custom the period of mourning for a close relative can last a week or more. Relatives come together to wail and keep all-night vigils. Otherwise the dead one has not been properly honoured. This expression of sorrow is meant to appease the spirit of the departed one and to ensure its kind feelings towards those left behind. The relationship of the living to the dead is a constant preoccupation of most Africans. Death itself is not feared so much as the spirits of the dead, which are believed to exercise an influence for good or evil on the living. The aim of ancestor veneration is to make sure that such influence will be good. The man whose father-in-law died, had returned to work only two days after the funeral. The translator asked him why he was not participating in the mourning activities. 'We don't practise much mourning in our family,' he answered. 'Some people do a great deal of wailing, and women show sorrow by sitting half-naked by the corpse. This goes on for days, but I don't find all that necessary,' The translator asked, 'Why not?' 'Beto zaba lufwa.' he replied with conviction. 'WE KNOW WHAT DEATH IS.'

Being a Christian, death was no longer an unknown for him. He knew that death had no power over him. He believed in Christ's victory over death. He could say with Paul, 'Death, where is your sting?' Simeon was a front runner in coming to that assurance.

9

Anna

Who Never Gave Up

Luke 2:36–38

We are still in Herod's Temple in Jerusalem.
Hard on the heels of Simeon's blessing and
warnings for the child Jesus, a very elderly lady
came into the sacred precincts. Her name was
Anna. Her pedigree was well-known. She was
the daughter of Phanuel of the tribe of Asher.
Moses had made a prediction about the tribe
of Asher that many have appropriated to
themselves. 'As thy days, so shall thy strength
be'(Deut.33:25). Anna was a living
demonstration that spiritual vitality can be
sustained to the end, however old a person
might be. She was the opposite of the person
of whom it was said, 'He died at 25 and was
buried at 65.'

A widow

Anna's days had been many. She was 84 years
old – a girl of 15 when Herod the Great was

born. She was in her fifty-second year before Herod became King of Judea. She had married but was widowed after seven years of life with her husband. Widowhood is one of the factors that Luke draws attention to in the women he describes in his gospel.

There is no indication that she and her long-deceased husband had children. She had lived scores of years as a lonely widow but without making her life a permanent requiem for her lost husband. She lived with a great sense of purpose right to the end. She was well known in and around the Temple, coming to it even when it was like a building site because it was being rebuilt by Herod.

An Intercessor

She never left the Temple; day and night she worshipped God, fasting and praying (Luke 2:36–38). Prayer was one of Anna's distinctives. She teaches us never to underestimate the prayers of the elderly.

Claus Reinhardt is a veteran German Christian, who after World War II served with a mission in Romania in its communist times. In recent days he tells his own story like this:

> From all outward appearances my old heart is ill, but spiritually it has become young and healthy! This period of time made me one of the happiest people.

Sometimes physically at the end of myself, and yet happy with my wonderful wife and children, I actually wanted to go into retirement. But Jesus Christ, my Lord, decided otherwise. Completely out of the blue I received a new task. Up until then I didn't want to accept the fact that I was growing older, and I rarely noticed other elderly people. I simply overlooked them, just like my age. And then Jesus gave me my own age-oriented assignment. I now get to care for elderly people in Romania! Together we get to experience along with Jesus the blessings of age!

What fascinates me about age? It is seeing with other eyes, feeling with their hearts and working with other hands! And it is with hands that my problems and my chances begin because I lost my right hand during the war when I was 17. My left hand had to do everything an entire lifetime, and today it is able to softly touch other tired, misshapen, emaciated and calloused hands. It lays across the shoulders of older people, giving them new courage and a zest for living, and it warms cold, worn-out hands. It can even direct a harmonica and coax a real smile from the teary, red-eyed faces of people my own age.

Age also brings us closer to Jesus in prayer. The challenges of age take care of the rest. How often long-forgiven sins rise again, and how often I have to tell myself and other old people that our sin is paid for, once and for all!

I knew Duncan Campbell, the man who was apparently the instrument that God used in the revival in the Isle of Lewis, off the west coast of Scotland in the late 1940s. He, however, attributed that remarkable work of God to two elderly ladies who for years had prayed for the salvation of their island home. The message of Anna is that all such as render service that is out of sight are known to and recognized by God.

A Prophetess

There are seven named prophetesses in the Bible and four who are only known as the daughters of their father Philip, the evangelist (Acts 21:9). Five of the named prophetesses have a genuine gift of prophecy and two are false prophetesses. Anna was a true prophetess and the first in the New Testament. She was all the more remarkable when we remember that centuries had passed without prophets in Israel and she was still more than 30 years earlier than the time when Joel's prophecy was fulfilled at Pentecost. Then, the gift of prophecy was bestowed on the daughters as well as the sons of the people of God (Acts 2:18).

It would be interesting to know when she received a call to be a prophetess or when she discovered that she had this gift. Was it before or after she became a widow? Everything we know about Jewish society would lead us to believe it was after she was made a widow. In that case, she discovered a gift that she did not know she had until after her husband died. She graduated from a sad marriage to a second ministry.

With people living so much longer today, sociologists are talking about us having a second adulthood. Shakespeare's seven ages of man do not cover the age range today. There are now:

The Tryout Twenties,
The Turbulent Thirties,
The Flourishing Forties,
The Flaming Fifties,
The Serene Sixties,
The Sage Seventies,
The Uninhibited Eighties,
The Noble Nineties, and
The Celebratory Centenarians!

Some have started jobs or activities they always wanted to do but did not have the time. Some because of sickness or disability or bereavement have had to make an inventory of their assets and plot a new course. They are even glad they had an illness, because, they say, that if they had not, they would never have walked away from a life that was crowded with activity but unsatisfying.

It need not be so. A longer life can be the call to a new discipleship in the second part of your life. If it is worked at physically, mentally and spiritually, with steady determination, it can postpone indefinitely any dreaded second childhood. Jesus can bring out another aspect of who you are, like Anna whose contribution to others was obviously greatly valued.

We do not have any record of Anna's prophecies, but it is clear that she had a reputation for her gift. When Anna spoke, people paid attention. At the same time as Simeon was blessing the infant Jesus and his mother and father, Anna arrived and was immediately caught up in what was going on. She too had spent her life waiting patiently for Messiah to come and deliver Israel and its holy city, Jerusalem. Her prophetic instinct led her to the same conclusion as Simeon. This child was Messiah.

A Witness

She also gave thanks to God and spoke about the child to all her friends who were waiting for God to set Jerusalem free. What she said, we do not know, but she spoke about the child to all, who, like her were waiting for God to set Jerusalem free. For Mary and Joseph this was yet another corroboration of the things that had been progressively revealed to them in the last year.

Anna is like the grandmother in a true story. On the morning when a family heard the news of their Grandmother's death, the mother had told the two older children before they left for school. They had cried a little and had been comforted and had gone away discussing soberly what life without Granny would be like. But the youngest, a four-year-old boy, was puzzled, and came and sat on his mother's knee to have it explained to him.

When at last he understood, he mopped his wet eyes with a rather soggy handkerchief, and smiled, struck by a wonderful idea. 'Golly,' he said, 'won't it be super for Jesus!'

There is no ageism in the Nativity. The old take their place and play their part with the young, all bound up together in the purposes of God.

10

The Men who Studied the Stars and their Findings

Matthew 2:1–12

Joseph and Mary and the child were eventually able to secure accommodation in a house in Bethlehem and returned there after dedicating Jesus in the Temple in Jerusalem. What a series of happenings had come to them unsought. The appearances of Gabriel to Zechariah and Mary; Zechariah being struck dumb and recovering speech when he said the name, 'John'; the angelic dream that allayed Joseph's fears; the providence of the census that brought them to Bethlehem; the visit of the shepherds on the very night of the birth with further confirmation that God was in all this; the recognition and prophecy of Simeon and Anna in the Temple; all this accumulation of circumstantial evidence gave them much to think about back in the house in Bethlehem in which they were staying. They must have been thinking it was about time for them to return to Nazareth. It was not to be – not yet!

'Soon afterwards, some men who studied the stars came from the east to Jerusalem' (Matt. 2:1).

An Impressive Delegation

They were 'Magi'. There is as much speculation about these gentlemen and their stars as about any other part of the Nativity story. There is no ground for supposing the Magi to have been three in number (as first suggested, apparently, by Leo the Great in AD450); or to have been kings. The first tradition appears to have arisen from the number of their gifts; the second, from assuming that they were a fulfilment of the prophecy. 'Nations will be drawn to your light, and kings to the dawning of your new day' (Isaiah 60: 3).

The Magi came from the East from the direction of Persia where there had been centuries of study of the stars and their courses. We see something of them in the book of Daniel where, in Babylon, they were kept as advisers to kings (Daniel 5:7). They studied and recorded what they observed about the movements of the stars, like our astronomers today. They also speculated about the significance of planetary movements for human life like our astrologers today. They had recently observed astronomical phenomena that led them to believe that a person had been born to be King of the Jews. Their sense of the significance of this made them decide to make the long journey to Jerusalem and pay their respects to this new royal personage.

We know from the Roman and Jewish historians, Tacitus, Suetonius and Josephus, that there was at this time, a growing conviction throughout the East, derived from ancient prophecies, that before long a powerful monarch would arise in Judea, and gain dominion over the world. World conditions had been so chaotic that it seemed that any change had to come from outside their current leadership. 'The dew of blessing falls not on us, and our fruits have no taste,' exclaimed Rabban Simeon, the son of Gamaliel. Another described the times as 'effete with the drunkenness of crime.' In that context, it is not surprising that the 'Magi' arrived in Jerusalem, the capital of Judea, looking for the infant that their observation of the stars had led them to believe had already been born.

Unusual Phenomena

There have been many attempts to try and find out what this 'star' was. One that has been around for 400 years or more is worth looking at to help us imagine what might have happened. I will describe it in layman's terms. There was a remarkable conjunction of two planets of our system a short time before the birth of Jesus that an ordinary eye would have regarded as a star of surpassing brightness.

In late May of 7BC there was a conjunction of Jupiter and Saturn in the constellation of Pisces, a part of the heavens noted in astrological science as one in which the signs denoted the greatest and most noble events. In October in the same year, another conjunction of the same planets took place, in Pisces. In December a third conjunction of these planets took place.

It is conceivable that the Magi observed the first of these conjunctions, in the East in May. If they then started their journey, they would have arrived at Jerusalem in about five months (cf. Ezra vii 9), in time for the second conjunction. If they set out from Jerusalem to Bethlehem in the evening, as is implied, the December conjunction, in 15 degrees of Pisces, would be before them in the direction of Bethlehem.

Something like that happened to these men. We cannot be more precise. No part of the text about the star implies that a miracle took place. It was something in the night sky that formed a pattern that their past experience made them conclude that it meant a royal birth in Judea. It was corroborated enough so that they felt they had to take out the best part of a year to go in caravan to Jerusalem and back.

An Awkward Question

In Jerusalem they asked around, 'Where is the baby born to be the King of the Jews? We saw his star when it came up in the east, and we have come to worship him' (Matt. 2:2). Unfortunately, they arrived when the succession to the throne in Jerusalem had been a matter in which several parties had a vested interest and Herod, the reigning king, was increasingly showing signs of having a terminal sickness. Suffice it to say here that five days before Herod died, he had his son Antipater murdered and changed his will for the umpteenth time. So the succession of the King of the Jews was a red-hot topic in what was virtually a police state ruled by a capricious king.

We are not surprised, then, to learn that, 'When King Herod heard about this, he was very upset, and so was everyone else in Jerusalem.' He was upset because it called in question the succession to his throne. The people were upset in case he might vent more violent behaviour on more of his unfortunate subjects. The king, however, remained outwardly very calm and decided to be party to this matter and not just let it end there. 'He called together all the chief priests and the teachers of the Law and asked them, "Where will the Messiah be born?" "In the town of Bethlehem in Judea", they answered. "For this is what the prophet wrote: 'Bethlehem in the land of Judah, you are by no means the least of the leading cities of Judah; for from you will come a leader who will guide my people Israel'" (Matt. 2:4–6).

It is interesting that he got so clear an answer so quickly. Apparently the Messianic expectations of the Jews were not far from the front of their minds, so this was not a difficult question for the experts. Herod had the answer to the visitors' question.

A Clandestine Meeting

He was not, however, going to divulge this information either openly or widely. Like the calculating man that he was, there was a piece missing that he needed to put in place. Herod called the visitors from the east to a secret meeting and found out from them the exact time the star had appeared.' This gave him the likely age of the child if it had been born at the same time as the first appearance of the star. If it was anything like the kind of phenomenon I have described above, the child could have been about six months old, by the time they arrived in Jerusalem. When he had this information, 'He sent them to Bethlehem with these instructions: "Go and make a careful search for the child, and when you find him, let me know, so that I too may go and worship him'" (Matt. 2:7–8). It was an unlikely story and the visitors were not taken in by it. They were among the keenest minds of that time. They saw that Herod had an ulterior motive, intending not to worship, but to kill this possible rival to the throne.

Indescribable Joy

As their caravan left and went south towards Bethlehem, the conjunction happened again where they could see it as bright as ever. It went ahead of them until it stopped over the place where the child was. When they saw it, how happy they were, what joy was theirs! (Matt. 2:10) The language is unrestrained. It was the moment of moments in their lives and they were not even Jews. Their years of study had led them to this unprecedented experience and there were no words to describe it.

An Appropriate Response

They went into the house, and when they saw the child with his mother Mary, they knelt down and worshipped him. This was behaviour only used for a god or a divine person like a king who was believed to be a god, as was common in Asia. We do not know what contributed to their conclusion that this tiny infant in a common home should be given the ultimate accolade of head-to-the-ground-worship. They were Gentiles and they would know from the Jews of the Diaspora in their own lands that Jews were monotheists. They worshipped the one who, they said, was the only God and not to be represented by any kind of idol.

Clearly, by some means, not spelled out for us, God had not left himself without a witness in the minds of these men and the journey to find Jesus was a climax in their search. It was a link between the stars in their courses in the heavens, their interpretation of them, the explicit guidance from Herod's sources and their finding the infant and mother that all combined to bring them to ecstatic joy and the impulse to bow down and worship the child born to be king.

In what kind of house did they find the little family? How large was it? Were they all kneeling at once or did they worship in turns. We do not know but I get the impression they were tall men. After the worship came the giving of unusual gifts. 'They brought out their gifts of gold, frankincense, and myrrh, and presented them to him.' They were gifts truly fitting for a king. They had come prepared. It shows how deeply they were convinced that their journey would lead them to the person they were seeking (Matt. 2:11).

The imagination of Christians from early times have seen in each gift a special significance; myrrh for human nature, gold for a king, frankincense for a divinity, or gold for the race of Shem, the myrrh for the race of Ham and the incense for the race of Japheth. These are only the product of people's imagination only mentioned because of their legendary influence and their influence on Christian poetry and art.

A Security Diversion

Any suspicions that they had about Herod's intentions were confirmed when God warned them in a dream not to go back to the court but return by another route (Matt. 2:12). Their need to change their route is the first intimation that Simeon's scary prophecy was not misplaced (Luke 2:34). Before the child was many months old there were those who wanted to get rid of him.

And so, in this manner, these august and mysterious persons disappear from the story. They leave behind much to think about. They are important because they bring another corroboration of the story of the incarnation from people who could not be charged with any bias. Gentiles for whom strict Jews had only contempt were drawn to witness this event and interpret the person who had been born as one worthy of worship and gifts of rare value.

Our Response

They make us question what our response

should be to this person, Jesus, who came with such evidences of his origin and purpose. They felt it was the response of worship that was demanded and they bowed low before him. We need to do the same.

11

Herod

The Slaughter of the Innocents: A study in violence

Matthew 2:16–18

In the story of the Wise Men we are introduced to the emotional atmosphere in Jerusalem towards the end of the reign of Herod the Great. When the men from the East arrived and asked their question, 'Herod was very upset. So was everyone else in Jerusalem,' but not for the same reason. Herod was upset because he feared another candidate for the succession to his throne. The people were upset out of fear that the unpredictable Herod might unleash a new spree of slaughter to combat any such development. Herod was a changed man in the last ten years of his reign. He provides for us a case study in violence.

In earlier life Herod could be magnanimous, courageous, and sometimes heroic. He was self-reliant and strong. He took on almost impossible challenges and pulled them off. He was clearly strategic and decisive and carried out ambitious projects with flair. Then he began to fear anyone or anything that might lead to his losing control. We saw signs of his ruthless side when he came to power, and immediately executed 45 of the 72 members of the Sanhedrin or Jewish Council. Today we would call him a control freak.

Manipulation Gone Wrong

A prelude to violence is often manipulation gone wrong. His total downfall, however, came in connection with the family he created. He made what he thought were strategic political marriages but they only widened the field of those who plotted against him. He married ten wives. By five of them he had 15 children. They and their mothers and other relatives conspired to secure the succession for their own branch of the family. It threatened to get out of hand. Herod became cruel and suspicious. No one was safe. The palace was full of plotting and intrigue and Herod executed several of his wives, three of his sons and several in-laws. He became ill and life in the palace in his last days was very unpleasant. He had hallucinations and Josephus describes his various sicknesses in graphic detail.

It did not help that he had to get confirmation of his successor from Augustus.

Because he was an appointee of Rome and not a king in his own right, the Emperor Augustus had a veto on any will that he made determining his succession. This led to a veritable circus of claim and counter-claim involving trips to Rome and trials in other places where Augustus asked some of his officials to investigate and adjudicate. Even his great friend Augustus, when having to arbitrate in a matter concerning Herod's sons, made the cruel pun, 'I'd rather be Herod's pig than his son!' (In Greek there is only one letter different between 'son' *huios* and 'pig' *huos*).

Easily Agitated

We are not surprised that when he learned from the Wise Men that the stars told them that another had been born who was to be King of the Jews, 'he was very upset and so was everyone else.' Another claimant to the throne of a sick and almost mad king was the last thing they needed. This alerts us to emotional instability as a precursor of violence. Though a great man, he did not manage his emotions well.

But he was smart. He knew about the prophecies of a Messiah who was to come. He was no fool. He actually thought in earlier life that he, himself, might be the Messiah. So he knew where to go to get information and cooperation. He went to the authorities that he himself had appointed and manipulated over the years and who were under his thumb. He was going to see to it that, if this was any Messiah, he would deal with him before it went any further. He did not baulk at setting himself up against what might be God's will.

Very Suspicious

'He called together all the chief priests and the teachers of the Law and asked them, "Where will the Messiah be born?"' They told him it would be Bethlehem. His next move was to have a secret rendezvous with the visitors. This unveils for us the kind of police state that he ran. Informers were everywhere. People were not allowed to meet unless the meeting was called by the authorities. When the visitors from the East did not come back to him, he enquired about them and was told they had gone back another way. He immediately assumed that it was a conspiracy. They had deliberately tricked him. Herod had a hysterical readiness to suspect the worst. You can see the wheels turning in his suspicious mind and grinding on towards the kind of false conclusion that a suspicious nature frequently reaches.

Angry

The text says, 'He was furious'. (v.16) Shakespeare makes Hamlet say that players who exaggerate the passion in their lines, 'out-Herod Herod'. We need to look further ahead in Matthew's gospel to discover the path that Herod was on.

Jesus later said, 'You have heard that people were told in the past, "Do not commit murder; anyone who does will be brought to trial." But now I tell you: whoever is angry with his brother will be brought to trial.' The root of violence is anger. Herod was on a dangerous path. There followed what we now call the Slaughter of the Innocents. 'He gave orders to kill all the boys in Bethlehem and its neighbourhood who were two years old and younger. This was done in accordance with what he had learned from the visitors about the time when the star had appeared' (Matt. 2:16).

For some time now, our society has been fed the idea that anger is good and it helps us if we give vent to it. Much of the psychological evidence is that expressing anger reinforces it and contributes to the deterioration of character. We cannot assume that what we used to call righteous anger is what we are exhibiting. It seldom is. The New Testament says that ' We should be slow to become angry because man's anger does not achieve God's righteous purpose' (James 1:19).

Anger is often making our problems someone else's and then stoking up a furnace

of blame that explodes in violence. It is a failure
to own what is our problem and take it out
on someone else. In fact, we are an increasingly
violent society because we are a society with a
lot of unresolved anger. So long as no attention
is paid to the diminution of anger, there will
be no diminution of violence.

Analogies

How did Herod, a man with such great gifts
and such solid achievement descend to this
unhappy end? Matthew does not make an
essay out of that. Instead he refers us to two
passages from the Old Testament and implies
that the stories there were of the same kind.

The first is from the prophet Hosea 11:1:
'I called my son out of Egypt' (Matt. 2:15).
This is a reference to the time when God
brought Israel out of slavery in Egypt and
through the Red Sea to freedom and the
promised land. The person who is in the frame
is the cruel despot, Pharaoh. Matthew is
implying that this kind of thing has happened
before and if you want explanations you will
get them from looking at Pharaoh. The
essential truth about Pharaoh was that he
progressively hardened his heart. In spite of
repeated opportunities to change and do what
God was asking through Moses, he hardened
his heart and drove on to his doom.

It was a perfect analogy for Herod and it

was no false comfort to Matthew's readers. It was saying that this is not the first time that this kind of thing has happened or this kind of monster has been loose in the world. Yet God's purposes were not thwarted then by Pharaoh and will not be thwarted now by Herod. This is clear evidence that we live in a world where evil is rife but does not prevail in the end.

The other analogy is taken from Jeremiah (31:15):

In this way what the prophet Jeremiah had said came true: A sound is heard in Ramah, the sound of bitter weeping. Rachel is crying for her children; she refuses to be comforted, for they are dead.

This refers to the time when Nebuchadnezzar came and took the people of Judah captive into Babylon. The prophet Jeremiah imagines Rachel, the best loved wife of Jacob, the father of the people of Israel lamenting the tragedy that is happening to her descendants as they are carted off to exile in Babylon. Yet Jeremiah writes of this tragedy as something that is about to be reversed. The next verse says, 'Stop your crying and wipe away your tears. All that you have done for your children will not go unrewarded. They will return from the enemy's land' (31:16).

Again it is saying that this kind of thing has happened before but the future is with God and Messiah will be his instrument.

Modern Examples

There are examples of such cruelty even in our time. Hitler, in Germany, Stalin in the old Soviet Union, Pol Pot in Cambodia, Milosevic in Yugoslavia, Saddam Hussein in Iraq are examples from the 20th century. Christians were among those who died. The texture of history for the people of God is often Herod-like but what is the last word? It is 'Herod died!' and what happened after that (Matt. 2:19). The Messiah lived and though he still had to watch out for Herod's successors, and eventually be crucified by them, his life was safe in God's hands. He rose again and lives for evermore.

The texture of the Cross is in the story of the birth of Jesus. Even if it is faint, the texture of the resurrection is there also in the preservation of Jesus. This is a message of hope for all of us who suffer at the hands of cruel and unprincipled people.

12

Matthew

The Account of the Tax Collector

Two characters contribute significantly to our picture of the birth of Jesus. They are the gospel writers, Matthew and Luke. We receive what they wrote as part of the process of revelation about the beginning of the Good News. There are some features of the story that are best tackled by looking at these writers and we begin with Matthew.

A Writer with a Clear Purpose

We are confronted at the beginning of the New Testament with what, at first sight to western eyes, is a dry list of the names that make up the genealogy of Jesus. On further examination, these name-heavy paragraphs have their own message which adds colour to the story.

They are a bridge from Old Testament history to the coming of Messiah. Matthew calls it literally 'The book of the generation of Jesus the Messiah the son of David and the son of Abraham (Matt.1:1 AV). He presents his genealogy in three blocks of 14 generations from Abraham to David, from David to the exile in Babylon, and 14 from the exile to birth of Jesus the Messiah. By this device he is hinting that the era he is now about to describe is the fourth part of the whole of God's purpose for the world. He uses these bold, broad brush strokes to signal his purpose in writing. He aims to convince Jewish readers that Jesus is the Messiah who will carry their history to its climax.

He mentions Abraham because he was the first to receive God's promise that his descendants would bring God's blessing to every family on earth (Genesis 12:1–3). He mentions David because he was unique. He is the only David in the Bible. He had been their greatest king about a thousand years earlier. After his time the rulers deteriorated and people increasingly longed to have another king like David. They were encouraged in this hope because God had promised David that when he died and was buried with his ancestors, he would always have descendants, and God would make his kingdom last for ever. His dynasty would never end' (2 Sam. 7:16).

David's dynasty did end in Jerusalem, with king Jehoiachin as Matthew states (Matt.1:11). Yet, in the centuries of foreign occupation that followed, almost all the prophets kept alive the hope that a descendant of David would still come and deliver them from their enemies. Every Christmas we read one example of what nearly every prophet foretells.

His royal power will continue to grow;
his kingdom will always be at peace.
He will rule as King David's successor,
basing his power on right and justice,
from now until the end of time (Isa. 9:7).

This expected deliverer came to be called the Messiah which means a person who is 'anointed' as King. Matthew repeatedly draws our attention to Jesus as the promised king over the kingdom of God.

A Deeply Sensitive Writer

He gives us a host of names each marking a generation. Some of them, like David were kings whose names we recognize. Others are quite obscure. The most surprising names in the list, however, were those of four women. It is rare for women to be recorded in formal genealogies. There are no women mentioned in the genealogy of Jesus given in Luke 3:23–38. In Matthew's genealogy, however, we have four women who might have been excluded by strict Jews.

Tamar was the daughter-in-law of Judah

(v.3). She was an alien, one of the Canaanites the previous inhabitants of the land promised to Abraham. After being shabbily treated by the family, she seduces her father in law by dressing as a prostitute and lying in wait for him by the roadside. She gave birth to twins. Phares the older of the two was the heir named in the list (Genesis 38).

Rahab (v.5) was also an alien and a prostitute when she comes into the story. In return for the help she gave to the spies and armies of Israel in the capture of the city of Jericho, she was welcomed into Israel and married to Salmon, and became the great, great grandmother of King David (Joshua 2:1ff).

Ruth (v.5) was a Moabite, who married her first husband when her Israelite in-laws had fled to Moab to escape a serious famine in Israel. Her father-in-law and husband both died and she and Naomi, her mother-in-law, were left as widows. News of a good harvest attracted Naomi back home and with great loyalty, Ruth went also. Ruth helped in the harvest and gained attention and recognition for her work from Boaz, a relative of Naomi's. Her mother-in-law was pleased to learn this because there was hope that as a relative he might marry the young widow. She advised Ruth on the night of the harvest festivities to act in a way that might have compromised Boaz. It was a daring plan, but it worked and

Boaz married her. In this way Ruth became the wife of the great grandfather of David (Ruth 4:18–22).

The wife of Uriah, is the fourth woman in the list (v.6). She was Bathsheba and the story is well-known. David committed adultery with her, and had her husband, Uriah, murdered to cover up the matter. He then married her and she became the mother of Solomon who succeeded David to the throne. What was behind this unique genealogy that included in it women who were normally shunned by others?

A Sense of History

Only Matthew tells us about the Wise Men who came from the East in search of someone who had been born King of the Jews. The last King of the Jews had been Jehoiachin, 600 years before (2 Kings 24:8). Ezekiel, the prophet had pronounced that there would be no successor 'until he comes whose right it is' (Ezek. 21:26–27). For 600 years the history of the Jews had been exile in Babylon, followed by a return to their homeland which was still a Province of Persia. Over the centuries it was conquered and ruled by different foreign powers.

Ironically, when Jesus was born there was a 'King of the Jews'. He was Herod the Great. He was not even a Jew. He was an Idumean.

By clever schemes he persuaded the Roman
Senate to make him 'King of the Jews' in 37BC.
He was escorted out of the Senate building in
Rome with Mark Antony on one side and on
the other, Octavius Caesar, later to be the
first Emperor of Rome. Herod went to all
lengths to retain the throne. The story that
Matthew tells of the slaughter of all the
children under two years of age, is only one
of his last attempts to get rid of a possible rival
and determine himself who should succeed
him.

Matthew subtly conveys how bogus were
Herod's claims by recording the opinion of
the Eastern Astrologers that one had been born
who was King of the Jews, even while he was
desperately trying to hold on to the throne.
As the story unfolds it is clear that the
protection of Heaven is over the newborn
King.

Fulfilled Prophecy
In the first two chapters of Matthew, as he
tells of the birth of Jesus he notes four times
that the events were a fulfilment of past
prophecies. First it was about the virgin birth.
'Now all this happened in order to make what
the Lord had said through the prophet come
true, "A virgin will become pregnant and have
a son, and he will be called Immanuel" (which
means, "God is with us")'(Matt. 1:22–3).

Next, the place of Christ's birth was a fulfilment of prophecy. '[Herod] called together all the chief priests and the teachers of the Law and asked them, "Where will the Messiah be born?" "In the town of Bethlehem in Judea," they answered. "For this is what the prophet wrote: 'Bethlehem in the land of Judah, you are by no means the least of the leading cities of Judah; for from you will come a leader who will guide my people Israel'"' (Matt. 2:4–6).

Then it is the flight of Joseph and Mary and the baby to Egypt. 'This was done to make what the Lord had said through the prophet come true, "I called my Son out of Egypt"'(Matt. 2:15).

After the killing of the children Matthew says, 'In this way what the prophet Jeremiah had said came true: A sound is heard in Ramah, the sound of bitter weeping. Rachel is crying for her children; she refuses to be comforted, for they are dead' (Matt. 2:17–18).

Finally the return of Joseph and Mary to Nazareth has this added note, 'And so what the prophets had said came true: 'He will be called a Nazarene'' (Matt. 2:23).

Matthew includes these three incidents that are only found in his gospel because they show how Jesus was seen to fulfil prophecies in the Old Testament. He tells the stories and he gives us the reference. He is at pains to present Jesus as the fulfilment of the promises of God in the Old Testament. About a score of times in his gospel he shows how events were the fulfilment of prophecy.

Yet this is no narrow Jewish patriotism. The universal relevance of the gospel keeps shining through. It starts with the story of the Wise Men who came from the Gentile or pagan East to see, recognize and worship Jesus. It is when we recall Matthew's own story that we realize why he wanted to include these items that are so distinctive of him. The answer is in the kind of person he was and the kind of experiences he had.

An Unpopular Tax Collector

Matthew was among those Jewish traitors who had bought a franchise that permitted them to collect taxes for the Romans, their colonial masters. What they collected was much more than the amount they paid to the Roman officials. People despised them for collaborating with their oppressors. They also resented the greed and extortion that they practised on rich and poor alike. These 'Tax Collectors' were shunned by most Jews. No one would have anything to do with them and so they gravitated to other people who were treated to the same social exclusion for different reasons. They were lumped together as 'Tax Collectors and Sinners' with prostitutes mostly making up the 'sinners' category.

Matthew lived in Capernaum, the same town where Jesus made his base. Jesus may even have paid his taxes to him. One day, out of the blue, Jesus invited Matthew to follow him as one of his disciples. That was a surprise to everyone including Matthew, but Matthew did not hesitate. He quit his job as a Tax Collector right away, but before he left, he threw a big feast in his house for Jesus and his disciples. Among the guests were many other tax collectors and prostitutes. Jesus was bitterly criticized for having anything to do with people like Matthew and especially for going to his party. The religious leaders asked his disciples, 'Why does your teacher eat and drink with tax collectors and prostitutes?' Jesus gave him his famous answer, 'Those who are well do not need a doctor, but only those who are sick. I have not come to call the righteous but sinners to repentance' (Matt. 9:9–12). Not long after this, Matthew became number seven or eight in the lists of the twelve Apostles (Matt. 10:3–4).

A Career Change

We would not have been surprized if Matthew had been the one chosen to keep the purse for Jesus and his disciples because of his financial skills. That, however, was given to Judas. Instead, Matthew, it would seem, became their note taker and eventually assembled his notes to write the gospel that bears his name.

Matthew was a Jew, but he had not been a good Jew. He had turned his back on his people by working for the Romans. He flouted God's law by the company he kept and the lifestyle he adopted. He probably resented the self-righteous attitudes of the Jewish leaders and people in refusing to have anything to do with him. When he became a disciple of Jesus, and saw how the Jews misunderstood and mistreated Jesus, he wanted to win them over. He made up for lost time and really worked hard at knowing how Jewish people thought. It was for them that he wrote his gospel. Like any good writer, the person he was, the experiences he had and the people he wrote for, controlled his material and his presentation.

He starts with the genealogy because he was writing for Jews in a way they would appreciate. He included the examples of fulfilled prophecy for the same reason. He included the four alien women for two reasons.

Matthew was about to describe the circumstances of the birth of Jesus. He reports that Mary was put in a compromising situation because she found out she was going to have a child by the Holy Spirit before she could be married to Joseph to whom she was engaged

(Matt. 1:18). This sensitive author gently reminds his readers that this was not the first time that those whom God chose and used, had faced similar circumstances in the past. It is interesting to speculate on where Matthew got the idea to include these women in his genealogy. Was it his own idea? Did he pick it up from listening to other Jews preaching on the subject? Or did he get it from Mary, the Mother of Jesus as parts of the Old Testament that had given her courage and confidence when things were hard to bear in Nazareth?

Matthew also remembered how Jesus had refused to exclude the lady friends in his old life, the prostitutes or 'sinners' as they were called. So, he structured his genealogy to express the same truth. With what gratitude must Matthew have recorded the words of the angel to Joseph 'She will have a son, and you will name him Jesus – because he will save his people from their sins.' It meant all his people and it meant all their sins and Matthew was glad.

13

Luke

The Researcher

There is even more exclusive material about the birth of Jesus in Luke's Gospel. When we recall what we know about Luke, again we find his very distinctive autograph in the material he uses.

The Sensitive Doctor

Paul tells us that Luke was a medical man, 'the beloved physician' (Col.4:14), yet there is no record of his treating or healing anyone anywhere. It was not that there were no sick people around. He writes about Paul and others healing people but he never seemed to get in on the act himself. He must have been a very diffident doctor. We are left to guess that his only patient may have been Paul himself who had a fairly severe recurring health problem (2 Cor. 12:7–9, Gal. 4:13,14). Even here, the degree to which he respected patient confidentiality is seen in the fact that we do not know either from him or from Paul himself the nature of Paul's illness.

Who better than a doctor to go into the antenatal and postnatal domestic details of a very surprised older couple and a very embarrassed younger couple who were each to have an unexpected child? Luke reflects God's interest in older people as well as the young. Zechariah and Elizabeth, Simeon and Anna would have been fine candidates for a Senior Citizens Club today.

Luke makes it clear that the women were as important as the men in God's purposes. Luke has a place in his world-view for poor and somewhat despised shepherds to be included in God's word to the world. He did not baulk at mentioning the fact that the young couple could only afford the paupers' offering of two young pigeons when they dedicated Jesus in the Temple (Luke 2:24). The doctor's touch is also seen in the interest he shows in how the children grew up (Luke 1:80, 2:41–51).

The degree to which Luke sensed the significance of all that happened around the birth of Jesus is seen in the emotional reactions that he describes in the childless couple coming to terms with having a child in their old age. We feel the emotion in the shepherds, first being scared out of their wits by the angels and then their insuppressible joy about the message given to them. 'The beloved physician' can also be detected in the fraught atmosphere that surrounded Simeon, Anna, Joseph and Mary, when the old saints realized that Messiah was there in front of them in the Temple.

The Careful Writer

It is apparent, however, that Luke shifted in his career from medicine to documentation as his primary task. He wrote the Gospel of Luke and the Acts of the Apostles, the biggest part of the New Testament. In this adopted profession of historian, he was still a very retiring person. If it had been left to him we might not even have known his name. It was left to others to put his name on his Gospel. The only notice of himself in Acts is the subtle change from the third to the first person plural in a few occasions. These are the famous 'We' passages in Acts that indicate that the author was present.

Luke presents himself as the researcher who wanted to give his reader a full, orderly and factual account of the things that had taken place in the coming of Jesus into the world. He begins, 'Dear Theophilus, many people have done their best to write a report of the things that have taken place among us. They wrote what we have been told by those who saw these things from the beginning and who proclaimed the message. And so, your

Excellency, because I have carefully studied all these matters from their beginning, I thought it would be good to write an orderly account for you. I do this so that you will know the full truth about everything which you have been taught' (Luke 1:1–4).

It is clear that he found gaps in the available documents that might confuse or deprive his intended audience. This audience is represented by a person called Theophilus whom he addresses with the respect he accords elsewhere to high Roman officials (Acts 23:26, 26:25). He wanted his account to be full and true and orderly for intelligent readers. He was ready to work hard to make it so.

We know that he met at least one of the other gospel writers. He was in attendance on Paul in Rome when Mark was also there (Col. 4:10–14). We can hardly doubt that there would be some discussion between them of their approach to writing their lives of Christ.

Both valued evidence from eyewitnesses as they worked on their subject. The result was that Luke presented as much as 40 per cent of material that is not in the other three gospels. The first of his exclusive material is his account of the birth of Jesus.

His Informants
The question arises as to how and where Luke found all this exclusive material. Paul implies

that Luke was not a Jew (Col. 4 10–14). He wrote mostly in good Greek but when he included material from Jewish sources his style reflects that origin. He does not tell us how he came to faith in Christ. His strong connection with Paul and the similarity of his language may mean that Paul led him to Christ. Paul's calling was mainly to preach to non-Jews. This means that the view of Jesus in Luke's gospel is the view of a non-Jew. We are not surprised then, when we see him including Simeon's note that 'the child was to be a light to reveal your will to the Gentiles as well as bring glory to your people Israel.' Equally it becomes clear why he wanted to include the doxology of the angels to the shepherd about 'peace on earth,' and not just in Israel. His genealogy of Jesus does not stop at Abraham. It goes right back to 'Adam who was the son of God' (Luke 3:38). The rest of his gospel keeps showing the universality of its message.

It is more than likely that Luke was not a Palestinian either. He himself tells us in one of his 'We' passages in Acts that he came to Jerusalem with Paul when he brought the money to help the poor believers there (Acts 21:19). Paul was then taken into custody in Jerusalem. For safety, he was transferred to the port of Caesarea where he underwent a series of trials. He was in detention for two years (circa 57–59AD) Luke is again with him when he is sent under escort by ship to Rome, joining him at the beginning of the voyage (Acts 27:1).

I like the view that Luke did his research in those two years when he was unable to help Paul much in prison. I can imagine him travelling up country in Palestine, asking around and interviewing as many people as he could find who still remembered details about the life of Jesus. Mary was probably among them, for scholars concede that only Mary could have given the details surrounding the birth of Jesus that we have in the first two chapters of Luke. If this was AD57 Mary would have been about 75 years of age. Alexander Whyte asks, 'Was it time for all these things that she had kept and pondered in her heart to start tumbling out?'

Was it the discovery of the extensive and indispensable role that Mary played that put him on to the scent of the other women whose story he tells in his gospel that the other gospels do not mention? Or was this just another thing he had learned from his sensitive and perceptive doctoring?

A Sense of History
Luke also sensed that history was in the making in the events that he was investigating up country in Galilee and Judea. We see in his

juxtaposition of the reign of Herod the Great, with the experience of Zechariah in the Temple that Herod was in process of rebuilding in a style and with a grandeur greater than either of the two previous Temples.

Again, when he comes to narrate the story of how Joseph and Mary came to be in Bethlehem for the birth of Jesus, he puts it in its historical setting. It was because the Emperor Augustus ordered a census to be taken throughout the Roman Empire that everyone had to go to his own town to be registered. The hand of God was moving the hand of the Roman Emperor to bring about his own great purposes for humankind (Luke 2:1). Later when he tells us about the preaching of John the Baptist the precursor of Jesus, he gives even more of the international, national, political and religious context in the time of the Emperor Tiberias (Luke 3:1–3).

Luke's historical sense can also be seen in his frequent use of the words 'Good News,' not used at all by John and very little by Matthew and Mark. The Greek word is EVANGELION and Luke introduces it in the message of the angels to the shepherds. 'Don't be afraid! I am here with Good News for you.' Luke and Paul almost exclusively use these words. Luke put the birth of Jesus at least in the same bracket with the Emperors of Rome.

Proclamations were made on their birthdays or other important occasion saying that the event they were celebrating was 'Good News' for the peoples of the world. For Luke the real 'Good News' was the coming of Jesus.

A Sense of Poetry and Song

Another very distinguishing characteristic in Luke was his ear for prophetic poetry. I cannot help thinking he was musical. In the space of the two chapters on the birth of Jesus we have four songs that we still know from the Latin words with which they begin. They are the 'Ave Maria' of Elizabeth (Luke 1:42), the 'Magnificat' of Mary (Luke 1:46–55), the 'Benedictus' of Zechariah (Luke 1:67–79) and the 'Nunc Dimittis' of the aged Simeon (Luke 2:29–32). All of these, Luke says, were inspired by the Holy Spirit in those who spoke them. For centuries now, all over the world, these songs have been sung in countless languages in church services. The person who recorded them for us was Luke. He was surely a man to whom prayer and worship had come to be very important in his new found life in Jesus Christ.

The message of Luke to us is that all of us, being the distinctive people we are, have our own understanding of Jesus that we can share with others. He shows us that the inspiration of the Holy Spirit does not relieve us from the hard work that any writer has to put into his writing.

> There is a Gospel according to Luke, but,
> You are writing a Gospel, a chapter a day;
> By all that you do and all that you say,
> Men read what you write whether
> faithless or true! Say, what is the gospel
> according to you?

14

A Boy's Dawning Consciousness

Luke 2:41–52

The scene shifts back to Nazareth after the little family had returned from their days as refugees in Egypt (Matt.2:23), but the story continues to unfold with the same theme.

A Normal Child

We know very little about the boyhood of Jesus, but what we know is significant. That he was a normal child is emphasized by the verdict Luke gives at the beginning and end of the single story we have of these years. He begins, 'The child grew and became strong; he was full of wisdom, and God's blessings were upon him.' He ends, 'Jesus grew both in body and in wisdom, gaining favour with God and people' (Luke 2:40,52). Physically, intellectually, spiritually and in his relationships, he progressed as do other children.

This is in marked contrast to the boy Jesus of the apocryphal gospels. He is mischievous, petulant, forward, revengeful. Some of the marvels told of him are simply aimless and puerile, as when he carries the spilt water in his robe; or pulls the short board to the requisite length; or moulds sparrows of clay, and then claps his hand to make them fly; or throws all the cloths into the dyer's vat, and then draws them out, each stained of the requisite colour. But some are, on the contrary, simply distasteful and inconsiderate, as when he vexes and shames and silences those who wish to teach him; he rebukes Joseph; or turns his playmates into young goats. Others are simply cruel and blasphemous, as when he strikes dead with a curse the boys who offend or run against him, until at last there is a storm of popular indignation, and Mary is afraid to let him leave the house.

How different is the Jesus of the gospel in his normality. Luther told a story about a godly Bishop, who had often earnestly prayed that God would manifest to him what Jesus had done in his youth. Once the bishop had a dream. In his sleep he seemed to see a carpenter working at his trade, and beside him a little boy who was gathering up chips. Then came in a maiden clothed in green, who called them both to come to the meal and set porridge before them. All this the bishop seemed to see in his dream, he himself standing behind the door that he might not be perceived. Then the little boy began and said, 'Why does that man stand there? Shall he not also eat with us?' This so frightened the bishop that he awoke. 'Let this be as it may,' says Luther, 'a true history or a false. I nonetheless believe that Christ in his childhood and youth looked and acted like other children, yet without sin.'

'Take notice here,' says the saintly Bonaventura, the thirteenth century Prince of Mystics, 'that his doing nothing wonderful was itself a kind of wonder. For his whole life is a mystery; and as there was power in his actions so was there power in his silence, in his inactivity and in his retirement....'

It seems that Joseph and Mary kept quiet about the revelations and adventures they had before and after the birth of their son. The attitude towards them in Nazareth did not encourage confidences like these. Apparently, they did not even talk much about it with Jesus himself.

An Annual Festival

Every year the parents of Jesus went to Jerusalem for the Passover festival. In this every springtime the Jews commemorated their deliverance by God from slavery in Egypt more than a millennium earlier. When Jesus was 12 years old, they took him with them.

From Nazareth, the journey was about 80 miles and took about four days. More than a million Jews from the country and from abroad converged on the capital. For size, it must have been something like The Haj when millions of Muslims converge on Mecca.

The age of 12 years was a critical age for a Jewish boy. It was the age at which, according to Jewish legend, Moses had left the house of Pharaoh's daughter; Samuel had heard the voice which summoned him to the prophetic office; Solomon had given the judgment which first revealed his possession of wisdom; Josiah had first dreamed of his great reform. At this age a boy of whatever rank was obliged, by the injunction of the Rabbis and the custom of his nation, to learn a trade for his own support. A year later he became a 'son of the Law'. He had his Bar Mitzvah and was presented by his father in the synagogue on a Sabbath.

A week later, when the Passover festival was over, they started back home. After his parents had set out, Jesus, without telling them, lingered for some days in Jerusalem talking with the teachers at the Temple.

Parents Panic over a Lost Child

When, after one whole day, Joseph and Mary were alarmed to discover that he was not with them, they searched for him among their relatives and friends in the crowd. When they did not find him, next day, they retraced their steps back about 20 miles to Jerusalem looking for him. Eventually on the third day, they found him in Herod's Temple having discussions with the teachers who were amazed at his intelligent answers. They wondered where he learned all this.

Jesus' Education

Jesus could read and write (Luke 4:16; John 7:15). He may have been taught by his parents or by a teacher attached to the local synagogue. His was non-formal education as it still has to be in many parts of the world today. We cannot suppose that he had many books, perhaps not any. He knew the Old Testament well and familiarly, better and more aptly than some people expected. Where he had access to it, we do not know. He learned what he knew in the home and workshop, in the desert, on the road, and in the market place. His parables show us how observant he was and how much he knew.

Jesus saw the life of woman in his mother's house, grinding at the mill, heating the oven by burning wood inside it, kindled with 'the grass of the field.' The leaven is at work in the dough where the woman hid it, and her son sits by and watches the heaving, panting mass. We may link all these parables from bread-making with what he says of the boy asking for bread. The mother fired the oven and set the leaven in the meal long before the child was hungry. 'Your heavenly Father knows that you have need of all these things.' Boys did not confine their demands to bread. They wanted eggs and fish as well. There was no end to their healthy appetites. They also wanted clothes, and wore them as hard as boys do. The time would come when new clothes were needed; but why could not the old ones be patched, and passed down yet another stage? And his mother would smile and perhaps she asked him to try for himself to see why; and he learnt by experiment that old clothes cannot be patched beyond a certain point. Sometimes moths ruined good clothes.

Nature is a classroom for Jesus. The eagle has the bird's instinct for carrion. The fox has its lair; the sparrow her nest; hens protect their chickens under their wings; dogs scavenge under the table; sheep and goats should be kept separately; pigs eat swill; snakes are vermin and need to be eliminated; wolves threaten sheep; fish are not always easily caught. All his knowledge of nature indicates that this was a great part of his schooling

Sunsets and cloud were his weather forecast. Grain grows so slowly that you think nothing is happening. Weeds are a menace, yet cannot always be taken out for fear of spoiling the wheat as well. Flowers can be beautiful beyond description.

We do not know how much of this knowledge came out when, at the age of 12, he talked with the teachers in the Temple, but something singled him out for special comment. His parents also were astonished at his performance.

A Revealing Dialogue

Mary remonstrated with him because he had caused so much worry to her and Joseph. She put it this way, '*Your father* and I have been terribly worried trying to find you.' This elicited a response from Jesus that indicated that this was a new subject between them. He said, 'Why did you have to look for me? Didn't you know that I had to be in *my Father's* house?' (Luke 2:49) They did not understand his answer. Mary had spoken of Joseph as his 'father'. Jesus spoke of the Temple as his 'father's house'. It would seem from this, that Mary and Joseph may not have talked to Jesus about the remarkable events before and after he was born. There are other reasons for thinking this as we shall see. Yet without their telling him about the revelations about his birth, Jesus was becoming conscious himself of his divine origins. From his own lips they heard him speak of God as his father, recalling what the angel had told Mary about the child being the *Son of the Most High* (Luke 1:32).

It was very rare for a Jew to speak of God as 'father'. Their view of God was so full of awe and respect that they sometimes did not even speak his name. The word 'father' for God is only used 15 times in the Old Testament. We should not be surprised that Mary and Joseph did not understand Jesus' answer. All that Mary could do was to internalize this further factor in the chain of revelations that she and Joseph had experienced all those years ago. 'His mother treasured all these things in her heart.' There did not seem to be more said on the subject.

A Happy Ending

'Jesus just went back with them to Nazareth, where he was obedient to them. He grew both in body and in wisdom, gaining favour with God and people' (Luke 2:51–52).

There followed about 18 more years of silence, before he began his public ministry. There were other children born to them, four brothers and at least two sisters. Since we hear no more of Joseph, we have to assume that Joseph died and Jesus succeeded him as the carpenter (Mark 6:3).

PART TWO

Introduction to John the Baptist

It seems clear that Matthew and especially Luke saw the work of John the Baptist as a continuation of the birth stories in their Prologues to the ministry of Jesus. They carried forward the threads from the story of his birth and boyhood right up to his Baptism and Temptation after which Jesus' own ministry takes off (Matt. 4:12–17, Luke 4:18).

From Private to Public

With the benefit of hindsight, we can see that a whole people had to be made ready to accept a view of how their hopes could be fulfilled and their fears overcome, that was radically different from the things they had believed for centuries.

What we have looked at up to this point was a series of private events that happened in the lives of inconspicuous people. They responded with differing degrees of faith to the relatively isolated experiences they went through. None of them had the whole story except Mary and perhaps Joseph and they found it difficult to make complete sense of it all (Luke 2:51).

We need, therefore, to watch carefully how the essentially private revelations given at the time of Jesus' birth, were made public before and in the life and ministry of Jesus. What Jesus brought to the world was drastically different from the mind set of the people of that day. The idea that God, as the Jews had learned to conceive him, was a Father and could have a Son, was as unacceptable to Jews then as it is violently denied by Muslims today. The Uniqueness and Unity of God was as entrenched and sacrosanct to them then as it is in the world of Islam.

The person who made the required change possible was John the Baptist and he did it in a very short six months. With two millennia of history between us and the Baptist, it is difficult to penetrate beneath the surface of the stories about him and grasp what was happening. There is little doubt that Jesus knew what was involved and how great the Baptist's contribution was, as we shall see in his assessment of John.

The Silent Years

Before launching into the events and the personalities, we need to have some idea of what did and did not happen in the 30 intervening years between the birth of Jesus and the beginning of his public work. We know that there was a security risk attaching to the child Jesus which made his family choose to stay in Nazareth in Galilee in the

North, rather than in Jerusalem or Judea in the South. There was also a social stigma arising from the nature of Jesus' birth from a virgin that gave the family reasons to lie low and keep out of any unnecessary public exposure in Nazareth (Matt. 2:22–23).

About Jesus, we have only one glimpse of him and his family when he came of age and was taken to the Temple in Jerusalem (Luke 2:41–52). We have noted that the idea that he saw God as his father, seems to have been a surprise to Joseph and Mary. This seems to say that not much had been communicated to him or to anyone else about the revelations that came at his birth. His cousins, James and John, were only introduced to the idea that he was the Messiah by the Baptist (John 1:35–42).

We have even less information about what happened to John the Baptist in these silent years. 'He lived in the desert until the day that he appeared publicly to the people of Israel (Luke 2:80). In spite of the family connection and the antenatal contact between Elizabeth, his mother and Mary the mother of Jesus, the Baptist did not know that Jesus was the Messiah until the day that he baptized him (John 1:31).

The Baptist seems to have had his own personal sense of call that drove him to preach and baptize(John 1:6, 33). We can probably assume that his parents Zechariah and Elizabeth died when he was young, because they were 'very old' when he was born (Luke 1:7). It is not unusual for a boy who has aged parents to grow up withdrawn. It is not unusual for someone who prefers the desert to the city or to farming country to be very reclusive. Maybe it was linked to a determination not to be a priest like his father.

The only traces of his beginnings are his life style and clothing which link with the prediction that he would be Nazirite. A Nazirite did not drink wine or strong drink and was a person a bit like the Elijah who would prepare the way for Messiah according to the prophet Malachi. (cf. Mal. 3:1, 4:5–6 with Luke 1:17, 76–79) The way he presented himself was new and personal to his own concept of his call.

This would seem to suggest that there were only trace memories of his parents and anything they might have told him. If they died while he was still very young, they might well have arranged for him to be brought up by a family or community who lived 'in the desert'.

Our task, then, is to explore how the Baptist made public what had so far only been revealed in private and a long time ago. The dramatic announcements that surrounded the birth of Jesus were that he was the Son of God, the Messiah and the LORD and that, in some sense, he would be a king like David. We will see these taken up and made public in the story of John the Baptist.

15

Going Public About the Messiah

Matt. 3:1–12; Luke 3:1–9

A Great Silence

There are 30 years unaccounted for in the life of the person we know as John the Baptist. All we are told is 'The child grew and developed in body and spirit. He lived in the desert until the day when he appeared publicly to the people of Israel' (Luke 1:80). There are, however, some deductions we can make from the facts that we do know.

We know that John's parents, Zechariah and Elizabeth, were very old when John was born (Luke 1:7). We can assume that they would die while he was still a boy, maybe even before he was old enough to be told about the unusual circumstances of his birth. Zechariah had been a practising priest and under normal circumstances an only son would have followed in his father's footsteps. Clearly he did not become a practising priest. He lived in the desert. Was this because of an arrangement that his parents made for him to be brought

169

up with some unknown family or community who lived in the desert? We know that there were communities who lived a life of seclusion in the desert near the Dead Sea. We can assume that his parents were trying to have him remain a Nazarite with uncut hair and abstain from alcohol (Luke 1:15). An arrangement with one of these communities would have placed him with people who respected such abstentions.

It is important that we try to imagine how much John had grasped at any particular time. We are looking at the very slow emergence of unanticipated concepts and events. John emerged from his seclusion and began to speak publicly to crowds of people. What he has to say is deeply rooted in the Old Testament. He has the garb, lifestyle and appearance of Elijah, the fiery prophet who challenged both king and people on Mount Carmel (1 Kings 18). His words are from the prophet Isaiah, when he was foretelling the equally important period when Judah was to be brought back from exile in Babylon to their own ancestral land.

It is the language of Isaiah that puts into his mouth the fact that it was the LORD for whom the way had to be prepared (Isaiah 40:3). The LORD was what Israel called God. Let's look at who John the Baptist was.

The Last of the Prophets, not a Priest

There had been no prophets in Israel for about 400 years. Luke makes it clear that the Baptist was in that line of succession by the way he introduces him and gives the context of his prophetic task. 'It was the fifteenth year of the rule of the Emperor Tiberius; Pontius Pilate was governor of Judea, Herod was ruler of Galilee, and his brother Philip was ruler of the territory of Iturea and Trachonitis; Lysanias was ruler of Abilene, and Annas and Caiaphas were high priests.' Each name tells a story. Luke differs in two respects from the way the Old Testament Prophets were introduced.

He relates the Baptist to two non-Jewish names. It was 15 years into the reign of the Emperor Tiberius. The Roman Empire was still the ruling power in the land. The reign of Caesar Augustus had already passed when John and Jesus fulfilled their calling. The era of prolonged peace under Augustus had given way to much more unstable times. Yet Luke is signalling that this prophet to whom the word of the LORD came had significance for the whole world over which Tiberius ruled. The Roman representative in the region was the Governor, Pontius Pilate.

The next three names tell us that the land that Herod the Great had ruled had been divided into several territories and given to two of Herod the Great's sons and one to another, Lysanias. They all reported to Pontius Pilate. This highlights the internal political context into which John had to speak and which Jesus had to face.

Annas and his son-in-law, Caiaphas, were from the High Priestly family that controlled matters religious and in particular had the monopoly of the very lucrative Temple affairs. Before he is finished, Luke will have shown that these secular rulers and religious priests were very significant players in the life of Jesus.

Having his own sense of call from God, he spoke of God having sent him to baptize with water. He indicated that he did not know that Jesus was the Messiah when he started his public preaching (John 1:6, 33). Luke describes him in the same way that prophets in Old Testament times were called by God, 'The word of God came to John, son of Zechariah, in the desert' (Luke 3:2). He stepped out into his country a fully formed prophet who had been taught by God in the solitude of the desert. When asked if he was the prophet, he said he was not (John 1:21). This is characteristic of his modesty. Jesus said he was a very great prophet (Matt. 11:9). The people also thought he was a prophet, the first for centuries (Matt.21:26).

John the Road Mender

John described the vision that he had received
in the desert in the words of an earlier prophet
of Israel, Isaiah.(Isaiah 40:3). The LORD was
about to come. John's task was to get the road
ready for him. He states frankly in words how
it is to be done. 'Turn away from your sins
and be baptized and God will forgive you!'
He states it also in pictures. Some he takes from
Isaiah. Some are his own images (Luke 3:4–9).

He borrows a picture of the preparation
that takes place locally when the ruler is about
to come on a royal visit. Roads and bridges
may have been neglected for years and be full
of ruts and pot holes. But when the king is
coming, no effort and no expense are spared
to get everything repaired and even new roads
are made where there were none before. The
fear was that if the journey was too difficult,
the King would pass them by and not come.
Or if he did come, heads would roll because
he was displeased with the way his territory
was maintained. We do not have quite the
same stir in the West when a Queen or a
President visits, but it is still a great occasion
in some parts of the world.

I saw great improvements undertaken
when Jomo Kenyatta visited certain parts of
Kenya in the 1960s. The country got a paved
road all the 300 miles to the coast, because,
among other reasons, Kenyatta liked to go

there. In Ghana in 1968 just after the Nkrumah era, I saw double gates on the roundabouts or traffic circles that could be opened to let his motorcade drive straight through the roundabout unimpeded. This is the picture John used to describe his role of preparing the way of the LORD.

It is not difficult to imagine how this translates into what God requires of us if we want Messiah to enter our lives or our communities. Jesus does not come unasked. We need to value his coming and make some essential preparations for it.

'Every valley must be filled up.' This speaks of our deficiencies and inadequacies. Jesus makes us whole by his own grace and power but we need to show that we want him to do it.

'Every mountain and hill must be levelled off.' This is a picture of the pride that keeps Christ from coming to us if we give in to it. We cannot keep thinking that we are great people and that Jesus is a great Saviour at the same time. How do we level off our mountains of pride? It helps to recognize how ungrounded our pride is. I am tempted to be proud of being a Scot. I had nothing to do with that. I like to think of myself as intelligent, but that comes from my parentage. What have we that we have not received? When we have discounted all of our false pride, we can come humbly to God. We can do better at honouring others. We can use even humiliations as stepping-stones down to a proper estimate of ourselves, if we take care not to react with resentment.

'The winding roads must be made straight!' The old version calls them 'crooked'. This is dishonesty and deceit. It keeps Christ from coming to us if we act a part or mislead people or behave dishonestly. A grocer was once asked why he would not go to church. He replied that when he went, he saw too many people there that owed him money. Crooked roads take longer and are much more tiring than straight roads. So are dishonest and deceitful ways. Let every person speak truth with his neighbour.

'The rough paths must be made smooth!' This could refer to the cruel streak in us, our spiteful self. When we are rough with people we lose our peace and most often disturb their peace as well. When we act considerately out of genuine concern for others, we get our peace back and so do they. Jesus keeps no company with cruelty.

The Person Who Was Coming

The seriousness of the Baptist's message to the people is in one little word, 'LORD' (Luke 3:4) They were to get the road ready for the LORD. This was the word the Romans used for their

Emperor. But it was the word that Jews used for God. I do not know what John's hearers imagined about how and when this LORD would come. John did not enlighten them. Jesus did so later. The people however knew that if it was the LORD who was coming, they had better pay attention and do what the Prophet was saying. They came in droves and were baptized.

The Baptist's Audiences

Crowds of ordinary people came out to John to be baptized by him. They came to him from Jerusalem, from the whole province of Judea, and from all the Jordan Valley. He sparked off a mass movement. It was significant enough for the authorities to send some priests and Levites to interrogate him (John 1:19–28). There were also Sadducees from the controlling party and Pharisees who laid special claim to be the true religious leaders (Matt. 3:7). Soldiers and Tax collectors came when they were off-duty (Luke 3:7–14).

John's Message – Be Baptized!

Up until then, baptism had only been for non-Jews who wanted to convert to Judaism. These converts had a variety of ablutions to perform. John's baptism was different in that he said that Jews themselves, of whatever pedigree, needed to be baptized. It was a direct attack on nominalism. This is the point of his references to Abraham and his children. 'Don't start saying among yourselves that Abraham is your ancestor. God can take these stones and make descendants for Abraham!'

There were three factors that fuelled the nominalism of John's audiences. It had a distinct racial side. Jews had intense ethnic pride. They were the people of God. Non-Jews were just so much fuel for the fires of hell. It had a religious side to it. They had the Law of God in their scriptures, his Temple in Jerusalem, and the Synagogues in every town. They also had the strict outward observance of ritual in their local Sabbath-keeping, their daily sacrifices and annual religious festivals in Jerusalem. John is saying that all this is useless unless you turn from your sin and are baptized.

Repent!

Baptizing Jews was a powerful way of saying that outward religious observance was not enough. Yet, in the end, baptism also is an outward thing, so people were flocking to him to be 'done'. They were making this just another way of substituting something outward for the inward change that was really necessary for them to prepare the way of the LORD.

It was at this point that John taunts them

with being snakes hopelessly scurrying before the fire. He imagines fields when they are set on fire to burn up the stubble or dry grass and the snakes wriggling and squirming, just to keep ahead of the creeping edge of the fire. 'You snakes!' he said to them. 'Who told you that you could escape from the punishment God is about to send?' It is a powerful picture, both humorous and tragic. It is humorous in the lengths to which people will go to avoid the one thing that is necessary; tragic in the consequences, for the fire will catch up with them.

His next picture is equally graphic. 'The axe is ready to cut down the trees at the roots, for every tree that does not bear fruit, will be cut down and thrown into the fire.' We know, in fact, that as far as their city and nation were concerned, many of their trees were felled by the axe. The leaders and the people who held out against John and against Jesus, perished in the siege of Jerusalem 40 years later. So, he emphasized, 'Do those things that will show that you have really turned from your sins.' Even baptism would do them no good if there was no fruit in their lives.

This makes it a very solemn thought for us in the 21st century. We have a vast problem with people who are Christian in name only, in Britain, Europe, the Americas, Australasia and Russia. If reality and integrity in the people of God are the precursors of Christ coming to renew his church, and heal the nation, there is a great work waiting to be done.

Salvation

We can approach the problem of nominalism in a helpful way, if we pick up a word used by John and his father Zechariah before him. It is the word 'salvation'. John says: 'All mankind will see God's salvation' (Luke 3:6). His father had prophesied at his birth that he would 'tell his people that they will be saved by having their sins forgiven' (Luke 1:77). This concept of salvation is central to all that John and Jesus brought to the world. Today it is sometimes parodied in jest. 'Are you saved?' says the comedian. The other person says 'Yes.' The comedian jests, 'Not from impertinence!' and imagines he has scored a point. Yet, salvation is what Jesus is about.

Before he was born an angel told his mother, Mary, that he would 'save his people from their sins.' He said about himself, 'The Son of Man has come to seek and save the lost.' Later Paul said it. 'God wishes everyone to be saved' (1Tim. 2:4). The Christian message is 'the way of salvation' (Acts 16:17). Christian preaching is 'the word of salvation' (Acts 13:26). The Christian gospel is 'the power of God for salvation for everyone that believes' (Rom.1:16). It is those who are 'saved' that are 'added to the church' (Acts 2:44). If a person 'neglects .. salvation,' there is no' escape' for that person (Heb.3:12).

Yet it is a comprehensive salvation, not anything trite or easy. Bishop Taylor Smith was once travelling in a railway carriage wearing all his Bishop's garb. A bold Salvation Army lass, herself dressed in her uniform, felt she should challenge the Bishop. 'Are you saved, Sir?' she asked. The Bishop looked on her with a kindly smile and said, 'Do you mean, "Have I been saved? Am I being saved? Or will I be saved?" and proceeded to open her eyes to the 'full' salvation that Jesus came to bring.

Unfortunately, there are many who have just not been told that there is a salvation that they may experience now. I have heard of titled people who attended an Alpha Course after being church goers all their lives. They discovered that there was more than they had been told or than they had heard and came to an assurance of salvation that gave them and their friends great joy.

The people force the Baptist to be more explicit about what kind of fruit he is talking about. We shall look at the detail in the next chapter.

16

The Moral Standards of Messiah

Luke 3:11–20

Specific Repentance

We have to imagine a mass of people gathering on either side of the River Jordan which is not very wide. John preaches to them dressed as a prophet like Elijah and thundering out their need to repent if they want to escape God's judgment. Many are deeply moved and begin to move down to join the Baptist in the river. It must have been strenuous work to immerse so many people at a time.

I recall the story of Paul Yonggi Cho the pastor of Yoidoo Full Gospel Church, the largest church in the world in Seoul, Korea. He was a dynamic 26-year-old pastor. Starting with just a handful of people in 1958 Dr Cho, with an almost unbelievable amount of zeal and hard work through days that began with 4:30 a.m. prayer services and finished past midnight, saw his congregation swell to about 3,000 members. 'I was young and puffed up and trying to do everything in my own strength'. he said. 'I carried the whole load of preaching, visiting, praying for the sick, counselling, writing books and articles, launching a radio ministry and administering everything from the janitorial service to the Sunday school and youth groups.'

But one Sunday evening in 1964, while preaching for the sixth time that day, and after personally baptizing 300 converts that afternoon, he collapsed in the pulpit and was carried out on a stretcher. 'The doctor told me that I had the worst kind of nervous breakdown and that if I wanted to live I would have to leave the ministry.' That crisis led to the changes that contributed to his church's phenomenal growth. Here I mention him only to show how strenuous baptising crowds of people would be for John the Baptist.

There were even Pharisees and Sadducees among those who came to be baptized. At his point the Baptist warned them that being baptized by itself, would not be enough. They needed to do things that would show that they had turned from their sins. If they did not, God would separate them from genuine penitents like chaff is separated from wheat and burned in a fire. John did not just work the line en masse. He was concerned about each individual. We see this in the responses of the people.

Some of the people asked him to be more

specific about what they were to do. The Baptist answered, 'Whoever has two shirts must give one to the man who has none, and whoever has food must share it.' This was a subsistence society with many desperately poor people. Jesus said that those who had spare food or clothing should share it with the destitute.

Not daunted and not apparently satisfied by this reply, some tax collectors came to be baptized, and they asked him, 'Teacher, what are we to do?' From what we know of tax collectors, they had more than enough food and clothes and they seemed to imply that there might be more for them to do. They were right and the Baptist shifted up a gear in his reply. 'Don't collect more than is legal,' he told them. They were to finish with injustice. It was generally understood that they could make what they liked from their tax collecting franchise, so long as the Roman official got what he had asked for. The system was set up so that they got their livelihood and their expenses out of surplus revenue. Jesus challenged them not to use their power to take advantage of people.

It was infectious. The idea seemed to be spreading that this matter of repenting had different implications for different people. Some soldiers also asked him, 'What about us? What are we to do?' He was even more explicit

with them. He said three things to them.
'Don't take money from anyone by force.
Don't accuse anyone falsely and be content
with your pay.' Soldiers often went without
pay from their officers for months. Occupying
armies saw to their needs by living off the land
they were in. They had the extra power from
the fact that they were armed and could
threaten people. Jesus said that repentance
meant not trading on their power either by
extortion or dragging people to the courts to
assert their will. More than that, he went to
the root of the problem. 'Be content with your
wages!'

The Dynamics of Confession

'They confessed their sins and he baptized
them in the Jordan' (Matt 3:6, Mark 1:5). We
have to imagine that John organized his
baptizing of people so that they confessed their
sins publicly to him, before he baptized them.
Without knowing more of the culture of the
people, it is difficult to imagine this. We can
believe that it was a new thing for those near
enough to hear the conversations between the
Baptist and each person. It was infectious. The
people and the tax collectors and the soldiers
all had something different on their conscience
and confessed it in the terms that the Baptist
had spelled out.

Sins at Work

We learn two things here. Our behaviour in our work place is included in God's assessment of us and there are specific temptations that are faced in different kinds of employment.

In these answers, the Baptist sent a signal that Messiah would not be departing from the Law of God that had been given by Moses. His standards would be the same. This was underlined by another daring confrontation that the Baptist provoked.

We need to picture the scene. Masses of people were pressing down the slope to the river and joining the line of people who were moved enough to do this kind of repenting. I imagine that one day while this was going on, Herod Antipas, the ruler of Galilee, rode by with an escort on his way between two of his many palaces. His curiosity was aroused by the large crowds so he drew nearer to see what was happening. Someone drew the Baptist's attention to the fact that Herod was coming. Everyone paused and things went eerily silent, waiting to see what would happen. This high-ranking man did not ask any questions, but that did not stop the Baptist from having something to say to him. He publicly denounced Herod for marrying his brother's wife and many other evil things. This is the story.

Herod Antipas

Herod Antipas, was a son of Herod the Great, who slaughtered the children in an attempt to eliminate the infant Jesus as a potential heir to his throne. He inherited the province of Galilee after the death of his father. Cruel, crafty and voluptuous, like his father, but, unlike him, weak in war and vacillating in peace. It is said of him that he was a man in whom were mingled the worst features of the Roman, the Oriental and the Greek.

Local rulers appointed by Rome, used to pay frequent ceremonial visits to the Emperor in Rome. During one of these visits to Rome, Antipas was the guest of his brother Herod Philip, another son of Herod the Great who was living in Rome as a private person. Herod Antipas became entangled by the snares of Herodias, his brother Philip's wife. He repaid the hospitality he had received from his brother by carrying off his wife. Everything combined to make the act as detestable as it was treacherous. Within the tortuous family tree of the Herods, Herodias also happened to be the niece of Antipas. She had a daughter, Salome, by Philip, who was now grown-up.

Antipas had himself been married for many years to the daughter of Aretas, Emir of Arabia, Antipas promised Herodias, on his return from Rome to make her his wife, and she exacted from him a pledge that he would divorce his innocent consort, the daughter of the Arabian prince. The people were scandalized and outraged. Internal family dissensions were embittered.

This is the man to whom John called out in his stentorian voice that it was not lawful for him to marry his brother's wife and went on to speak of a number of other evils that he had perpetrated. There must have been anxious gasps from the crowd. When the royal party galloped off, there would be a feeling that what the Baptist had done would result in serious consequences.

Rising Hopes

In the middle of his narrative, Luke says, 'People's hopes began to rise, and they began to wonder whether John himself might be the Messiah.' Antipas was not a popular ruler. The sight of someone daring to stand up to him might well have put ideas into the heads of some people. Perhaps John himself was Messiah who would really begin to set things right in their country. It was not surprising.

John, however, would have none of it. He said immediately to all of them, 'I baptize you with water, but someone is coming who is much greater than I am. I am not good enough even to untie his sandals. He will baptize you with the Holy Spirit and fire. He was not only unequivocal about his own inferior status, he hinted at the fact that there was another blessing to come that Messiah would bring. He would baptize them with the Holy Spirit.

How his listeners would understand this is difficult to gauge. It is likely, however, that their minds would go back to some of their ancestors on whom it was said that the Spirit came – Joseph, Moses, Joshua, Samson, David, Isaiah, Ezekiel, Daniel. They were mostly leaders, rulers or prophets. They may even have picked up passages that they had heard read from the scripture scrolls in their synagogue in Isaiah, Ezekiel and Joel that spoke of a more general 'pouring out' of the Spirit, even 'on all flesh' according to Joel (Joel 2:28–29). That would be remote from their experience. They would understand, however, that anything about the spirit would be about what happened in peoples' hearts. John would be heard as saying that Messiah would change people's hearts and not just their law-keeping. The Law was the source of the moral standards that John preached. The motivation to keep the Law had to come from the Holy Spirit.

This is another first. John was the first to speak of the baptism of the Spirit. The angel Gabriel had told John's father that his late-born son would be filled with the Holy Spirit from his birth and that as an adult, he would go before the Lord in the Spirit and power of Elijah. Luke says of his earlier life in the desert that he became strong in spirit. John would know personally more about the Spirit than his hearers. For them it was still something to look forward to.

Repercussions

The Baptist's preaching invaded a social institution when he asked for an ethical tax-collecting policy. He could look like a threat to the security of state when he talked about the behaviour of the military. Some time later, therefore, Herod Antipas sent a detachment of troops to arrest John and put him in prison in the forbidding fortress of Machaerus in the desert on the east side of the Dead Sea. This was a highly unpopular move, but there was little the people could do about it. Later, when Herod's army suffered a humiliating defeat at the hands of Aretas, his former father-in-law, the people said it was the judgment of God for the way he treated John the Baptist.

17

The True Origin of Messiah

Matthew 3:13–17, Luke 3:21–22

One day, after all the people had been baptized, John saw a familiar figure coming down the river bank towards him. I say, 'a familiar figure' but we do not know if Jesus and John ever met before this day.

The Baptist later told some of his disciples that he had not known who the Messiah would be, but God, who sent him to baptize with water, had told him that he would see the Spirit come down and alight on a man and he would be the one (John 1:31–34). That means that either the Baptist knew his second cousin, Jesus, but did not know anything about his being the Messiah, or, John had not met Jesus at all. If we look at all we are told in the gospels, the first of these alternatives is the most likely.

We know that Joseph and Mary and some of their family went down, every year, from Nazareth in the north to Jerusalem for the Passover festival. It would seem likely that John who lived in the South might well have been taken to the same festivals and would look out for their relations from the North. It would have been a natural way for them to meet. We do not know what they thought about each other, but it would seem from what follows that John was very impressed with Jesus.

A Different Candidate

So, the Baptist, one late afternoon, saw this familiar figure coming down the river bank towards him. Matthew indicates that it was just after John's encounter with some Pharisees and Sadducees who had come to be baptized but without grasping what it was really about.

Jesus presented John with a different problem. When he asked to be baptized, John tried to make him change his mind. 'I ought to be baptized by you,' John said, 'and yet you have come to me!' (Matt. 3:14) Something about Jesus made John treat him differently from all the others. It raises an interesting question. Had John himself been baptized? Had he baptized himself? Others have.

When Baptist churches began in England in 1608, Cambridge-educated John Smyth baptized himself. He had become convinced about believers' baptism and went to Holland to meet with people of this persuasion and be baptized by them. He could not find a group with the same understandings as his own, so he baptized himself and was called the 'Se-Baptist' and went on to baptize others.

John the Baptist had probably not been baptized himself. He claimed that God sent him to baptize with water (John 1:33). When Jesus approached him, there was a marked change of tone in John. He said that he himself was the one needing baptism. This seems to indicate that he had some sense that Jesus was so different from all the other people who had come to him that he was in a special exempt category.

Jesus, however, was persistent and insistent, and yet he seems to recognize why John had the problem. He said, 'Let it be so for now. For in this way we shall do all that God requires.' So John agreed and baptized Jesus. There followed another whole series of surprises. While he was praying, heaven was opened, and the Holy Spirit came down upon him in bodily form like a dove. And a voice came from heaven, 'You are my own dear Son. I am pleased with you' (Matt. 3:13–17).

Often we have a picture of a person before we ever meet them. We get this from letters, phone calls, photographs, from things said by other people. Then when we meet them it can be quite different. It was like that with John and Jesus. Let us list, in the order in which they occurred, the surprises that came to John that momentous day.

Jesus wanted to be baptized

This was before John knew that Jesus was Messiah (John 1:33). What made John raise an objection? It was very different from John's very direct and uncompromising treatment of everyone else who came to him. Did it have to do with the confession requirement? Did he just see and sense that this was an exceptionally good person? Did he interrogate him and become more astonished by the minute by replies that showed he had not sinned? Did he, in fact, from previous contacts, know him as an exceptionally good person that even he could not come near in character? We would love to have answers but all we get from the gospels are more questions at this point.

Why did John say, 'I ought to be baptized by you yet you have come to me?' Had he who had baptized thousands, never been baptized himself? Did that signify that he stood over against all these sinners as a person apart, but uncomfortably so? Was it when Jesus stood in front of him, that his own sin and need of cleansing surfaced and made him want Jesus to baptize him?

Whatever the explanation, it was a moment of great shock and confusion for John. Jesus seemed in perfect command of the situation and persuaded him to do the baptism explaining, 'In this way we shall do all that

God requires.' The key word seems to be 'all'. John was clearly concerned about righteousness but this apparently was outside his concept of righteousness.

Here we begin to see the difference between John and Jesus. John was the unbaptized Baptizer and Jesus was becoming the baptized Messiah. Up to this point, John had no thought of being baptized himself. He was the Baptizer, the censor of sinners, not the sympathetic fellow sinner. Here he begins to be confronted with the difference between the Messiah he had been imagining and talking about and the real Messiah that God was showing him.

He was severe. Jesus was sympathetic. John had the drive to baptize others. Jesus wished to be baptized, as if a sinner himself. He assumed the position of solidarity with the sinner. Rather than the position of critic and judge. Love not moral indignation was guiding Jesus' actions. When we think of it, can we really imagine sinlessness being so conscious of itself that it adopts a policy of keeping aloof from sinners? Surely not!

Jesus' baptism might have created misunderstanding just as his keeping company with tax collectors and prostitutes did. Being misunderstood served his purpose better than adulation. It is this grace of identification with us that made up the 'all' that God required in righteousness. John's idea of righteousness was ultimately narrow, severe and legalistic. He had not understood that love is the fulfilling of the law. He was learning fast as he went down into the River Jordan with Jesus. His second surprise was:

The Spirit was like a Dove

Jesus prayed as he was baptized. He was very much in touch with God. 'Then the heavens opened and the Holy Spirit came down upon him in bodily form like a dove' (Luke 3:21–22). This was the way in which God showed John that Jesus was Messiah as he, John, had been promised. It must have added to his confusion. All the Baptist's language shows us that the Spirit of stormy wind and fire with judgment as its purpose was what he would have expected. Instead, he saw the Spirit as a dove, like the bird that brought the olive twig to Noah after the judgment of the flood. It symbolized judgment past and God's favour restored (Gen. 8:9–19).

Messiah was the Son of God and yet a Servant

Even while John was coping with that shock, another was on its way. A voice spoke from heaven, 'You are my Son whom I love. With you I am well pleased.' So far it had only been revealed privately to Mary, his Mother, that her child would be 'the Son of the Most High God' (Luke 1:32). Now it was revealed publicly to John by the cleaving of the heavens over Jordan, the descent of the Spirit as a dove and the voice which said, You are my own dear Son. I am pleased with you.'

John has shown us that he was very familiar with the prophet Isaiah. He saw himself as 'the voice of one crying in the desert. "Prepare the way of the Lord, make a straight path for him." in Isaiah 40. Now the voice moves on to what he would recognize as Isaiah 42:1–3. The Divine Son of Psalm 2 is the Suffering Servant of Isaiah 42, who will not shout or cry out or raise his voice in the streets. A bruised reed he will not break and a smouldering wick he will not snuff out.

To put it bluntly, the Baptist had said that the one who would come would be high and mighty. John would not even qualify to be a slave in his household, who would untie the thongs and take the sweaty sandals from his feet. The voice from heaven was forecasting that the one to come would himself take a towel and basin and wash all his disciples' feet. Could he have been more different?

Jesus was Messiah

All wrapped up in that deluge of revelations was the central surprise to the Baptist. He had seen the Spirit descend on him. Cousin Jesus was Messiah! Later Jesus gave a clue as to what his being baptized meant. He spoke of his death as being the baptism with which he was about to be baptized (Mark 10:38). You cannot get closer identification with sinners than to bear their sins on a cross. John was learning fast as he went down into the River Jordan with Jesus.

Conclusion

It was a day of surprises, even shocks, for John, but a day of great joy for us. If we have suffered at the hands of such austere prophets who describe us as John did, as snakes scurrying before the fire, let us take heart. If our conscience has made us shudder at the thought of the axe thudding into the base of our unfruitful tree, we need to be encouraged. If we have been alarmed because we see much of our lives being blown away as chaff before the wind, it has only been to prepare the way for a gentler Lord than we realized was there. We find him at the beginning of his ministry, standing beside us in our Jordan. He is sympathetic to us, ready to work for and live for us. In time he will die for us, rise to be forever alongside us till he makes us what he wants us to be. Let us believe in his love and trust in his death for us. Let us begin to make the change and follow him, as some of John's disciples did at the time, finding a more motivating faith and a fuller life than they had experienced in following John.

John met Jesus and recognized he was Messiah, reluctantly, as we see in the rest of the story. Some of his followers decided to stick with John long after he was dead. They stuck to his harsh message and knew nothing of what it was to be baptized with the Spirit. We can do that also and many do. We may even know some such very judgmental people. Today, let John introduce us to his unexpected Messiah, and we too will be changed. For none can meet him and go away the same.

18

Witness to Messiah

John 1:6–9,15,19–37, 3:22–30, 5:33–36,
10:40–41

Time for Reflection

The experience when John baptized Jesus must
have been momentous both for the Baptist and
for Jesus. Inevitably, there must have been
extended conversations between the two
cousins. They both needed time to think and
process this earth-shattering event.

Jesus was prompted by the Spirit who had
descended on him as he came up from the
water, to go south into the desert to reflect. I
could imagine that John advised him to do
that, since he knew the benefits of seclusion
in the desert more than anyone. If he did, then
the Spirit also said go and he went.

It was a time of temptation. Jesus really
had to wrestle with what he was going to do
now that God had spoken to him. What
difference did it, should it make? What should
he do next? What should he do later? He spoke
about this later and told his disciples that the

temptation had come from the devil along three lines. The first was the temptation to misuse his power as the Son of God for personal gratification. He repudiated that. He was tempted to engage in spectacular public displays to mesmerize the people. He turned that away. He was presented with the possibility of international power and rule greater than that enjoyed by the Roman emperor if he would compromise his loyalty to God, his father. It left him cold (Matt. 4:1–11, Luke 4:1–13).

For the Baptist, during the five or six weeks when Jesus was away in the desert, this was time to reflect on the revelation he was given, while standing with Jesus in the waters of the Jordan. He was used to reflecting. He was close to God. It is clear from the sequel that he continued in the secret place waiting on God to find out what all this meant.

We are indebted to John, the Apostle, for an account of what followed. He himself was present. Later in life when he felt he should supplement what the first three gospel writers had written, he decided that this gap between the baptism of Jesus and the Baptist's imprisonment by Herod should be filled in.

Interrogation by the Authorities
Clearly, word was carried back to Jerusalem, the capital, about the activities of John the

Baptist. We would not be surprised if Herod Antipas, indignant about being censured by the Baptist for his adultery, did not himself send back a message to the chief priests that something needed to be done about John. He could well allege that he was being subversive.

Wherever the prompt came from, the Jewish authorities in Jerusalem sent some priests and Levites to John to interrogate the Baptist. If they were old enough, some of them might have known John's father, Zechariah, who served as a priest in the Temple in Jerusalem 30 years previously. The thrust of their interrogation was to examine his credentials.'Who are you?' they asked. John saw what they were trying to get at and was open with them.'I am not Messiah,' he said.'Who are you, then?' they asked. 'Are you Elijah?' There had been a prophecy in the Old Testament that someone like their earlier prophet Elijah would come to prepare the way for Messiah (Malachi 4:5). They wondered if the Baptist was Elijah incognito. John replied again in the negative.

They then moved to an older prophecy that God would one day send a prophet like a second Moses (Deut.18:18). 'Are you the Prophet?' they asked. Again he denied it. In exasperation they demanded, 'Then tell us who you are. We have to take an answer back to those who sent us. John gave them the same answer he gave to everyone, quoting the prophet Isaiah: "I am the voice of someone shouting in the desert: Make a straight path for **the LORD** to travel!'" They were none the wiser.

They took another tack, 'If you are not the Messiah nor Elijah nor the Prophet, why do you baptize?' To this John answered, 'I baptize only with water, but among you stands one you do not know. He is coming after me, but I am not good enough even to untie his sandals' (John 1:19–27).

A Torrent of Revelation

All this happened on the last day before Jesus came back from the desert, having emerged unscathed from his temptations. The next day John saw Jesus coming towards him, back from the desert. He pointed and out of the blue, said, 'There is the Lamb of God, who takes away the sin of the world! This is the one I was talking about when I said, "A man is coming after me, but he is greater than I am, because he existed before I was born." I did not know who he would be, but I came baptizing with water in order to make him known to the people of Israel.' And John gave this testimony: 'I saw the Spirit come down like a dove from heaven and stay on him. I still did not know that he was the one, but God, who sent me to baptize with water, had said to me, "You will see the Spirit come down and stay on a man; he is the one who baptizes with the Holy Spirit." 'I have seen it', said John, 'and I tell you that he is the Son of God.'

John as a Witness

John's gospel presents John the Baptist as the first witness to Jesus Christ (John 5:33–35). The content of his witness is amazing and shows that the six weeks that Jesus was away in the desert being tempted, allowed John to put many things together and reach startling conclusions.

The Son of God

We are not surprised that he should witness to the fact that Jesus was the Son of God. That had been what the voice from heaven had said. But have we given that the weight it deserves. If we were asked the question, 'Who was the first to confess that Jesus was the Christ, the Son of God?' Most of us would probably say, 'Peter, at Caesarea Philippi.' But we would be wrong. It was John the Baptist. More than that, however, he developed the implications of that fact by twice stating that Jesus existed before he, the Baptist, was born. 'He cried out, "This is the one I was talking about when I said, 'He comes after me, but he is greater than I am, because he existed before I was born'"' (John 1:15,30). He declares the pre-existence of Christ.

It is no accident that John, in his gospel, interweaves the story of John the Baptist with his highly theological prologue. We learn later in chapter one that the apostle John, was a disciple of the Baptist and it was the Baptist who introduced him to Jesus (John 1:35–37). So his majestic opening, 'In the beginning was the Word; and the Word was with God and the Word was God; the same was in the beginning with God,' is a hark back to John the Baptist's discovery of this truth in the period after he baptized Jesus (John 1:1–2 AV).

The Lamb of God

In some communion services the people say three times, 'Lamb of God you take away the sins of the world, have mercy on us!' Where did these words come from? Only from John the Baptist. They are not in any other gospel. Paul and Peter in all their letters each have the same thought only once about Jesus (1 Cor. 5:5, 1 Peter 1:19). Jesus is called the lamb nearly forty times in the book of Revelation.

Since the Baptist was speaking long before the crucifixion of Jesus, he must have been drawing his understanding from the Old Testament prophet, Isaiah, in whose words he articulated his own call (Isa. 40: 3–5). 'He endured the suffering that should have been ours, the pain that we should have borne...... All of us were like sheep that were lost, each

of us going his own way. But the LORD made
the punishment fall on him, the punishment
all of us deserved. Like a lamb about to be
slaughtered, like a sheep about to be sheared,
he never said a word' (Isaiah 53:5–7).

The Light of the World

Matthew gives us this metaphor about Jesus
and it becomes a recurring theme in the New
Testament. Yet when we turn to the gospel of
John, we see that the concept originated with
the Baptist. 'God sent his messenger, a man
named John, who came to tell people about
the light, so that all should hear the message
and believe. He himself was not the light; he
came to tell about the light. This was the real
light – the light that comes into the world and
shines on everyone' (John 1:6).

John the Baptist is himself described as a
burning and shining light (John 5:35),
anticipating the fact that Jesus said that his
disciples would also be the light of the world
(Matt. 5:14–16).

The Bridegroom

Jesus is called the 'bridegroom' and his church,
his 'bride' in several places in the New
Testament. The first to use it was the Baptist.
It was on an occasion when some of John's
disciples complained to him about the
popularity of Jesus. With great modesty and

deference he responded, 'No one can have anything unless God gives it to him. You yourselves are my witnesses that I said, "I am not the Messiah, but I have been sent ahead of him." The bridegroom is the one to whom the bride belongs; but the bridegroom's friend, who stands by and listens, is glad when he hears the bridegroom's voice. This is how my own happiness is made complete. He must become more important while I become less important' (John 3:29–30).

The Holy Spirit
Already we have seen that the Baptist is the one who announces the impending arrival of the new era of the Holy Spirit. He said that Jesus would baptize his genuine followers with the Holy Spirit and foreshadowed the day of Pentecost three years before it happened.

There are so many new notes in John's theology that one rather unsympathetic commentator had to write, 'If any man could be said to be, historically speaking, indispensable to the beginnings of the movement we call Christianity, that man was John the Baptist.' He is the first to speak of the kingdom of heaven. So many ideas that are commonplace to us as Christians we derive, in fact, from John the Baptist.

He was a true forerunner preparing the way, sowing the seeds of new truth that, having germinated after he planted them, bore fruit in the life and work of Jesus and in the history of the church. He was an original. He was no copy. One writer has said, 'John the Baptist set in motion a dynamic that was much more consequential than Herod could ever have imagined. The movement he began was ultimately to shake the foundations of the Empire itself. The figure of John the Baptist stands at the beginning of Christianity, which for good or bad, was to preside over the dissolution of the Empire and, strangely enough, to preserve that Empire's heritage for almost 2,000 years. His was more than an individual's struggle with God, as profound as that may be. It was the struggle of a people grappling with itself in such a way that it set a course of events that, even in the 21st century has not come to its fullness of time.

There is an ironic note that needs to be heard from the gospel of John. It is a statement of the people who lived in one of the places where John had baptized people three years before. 'John performed no miracle,' they said, 'but everything he said about Jesus was true' (John 10:41).

We are impressed with how rounded John's theology so quickly became. His work lasted only about six months, yet, most of what we believe as Christians was already there in embryo. He was implicitly Trinitarian: as soon as he said Jesus was the Son of God, he implied 'the Father'. At Jesus' baptism we have the voice of the Father from heaven, the presence of the Son in the river and the Spirit descending like a dove. It is a great mystery, as God must be to mere men, but the mystery is first hinted at by John.

He was gaining a world outlook, so different from the exclusive ethnic ideas that controlled his people at that time. 'All mankind was to see the salvation of God' (Luke 3:6). The Lamb of God was to take away the sin of the world (John 1:29). Though a Jew and a priest's son, he had no narrow Judaism. He saw the whole world as the object of God's working in salvation.

He had a most thorough idea of man's need. Humankind were condemned as sinners to the judgment of God; needed to confess their sins; to repent of them; to be baptized; to receive forgiveness and live a life consistent with these steps.

19

The Kingdom of God

(Matthew 11:1–19, Luke 7:18–35)

An Uneasy Coexistence

At Bethany, beyond Jordan, the Baptist introduced Jesus as Messiah and the Lamb of God to some of his own disciples. He raised no objection when they seemed to become more interested in Jesus than in him (John 1: 28–42). The Baptist did not himself follow Jesus but continued to work with his own disciples. We do not know if he referred to Jesus publicly as the Messiah. We do know that he spoke about him privately, in a positive way (John 3: 25–30, 4: 1–2). The Baptist and his disciples operated mostly in the South, in Judea.

When Jesus and his disciples were in the same area, there were signs of friction between the two sets of disciples. There was natural tension when Jesus seemed to be more popular and attracted more people to be baptized. When Jesus heard about the tension, he removed himself to Galilee in the North (John 1:43, 4:3).

John's disciples fasted often and lived an austere life, but Jesus' disciples did not (Mark 2:18–22). John taught his disciples to pray but we do not know how (Luke 11:1). We know that when Jesus' disciples asked him to do the same, he taught them what we know as the Lord's prayer. Could John have prayed the Lord's prayer? Probably most of it but perhaps not the prayer for forgiveness as we forgive those who sin against us. John did not perform miracles (John 10:40–41), whereas from the beginning Jesus made wonderful things happen.

If we follow the account in John's gospel, Jesus made a name for himself in the cleansing of the Temple. He spoke to leaders like Nicodemus and put the Samaritan woman and her townsmen on the straight and narrow path of salvation. It must have pleased John, if he heard about these things and it would appear that his own disciples made sure he did. What he would have thought about Jesus turning water into wine at the wedding, or healing the son of the government official, may have been a different matter.

The Baptist's disciples continued after he died. They were still around many years later. Apollos knew only the baptism of John and he was brought up in Alexandria, in Egypt.

Twelve more were found by Paul, in Ephesus, far away from Jordan (Acts. 18:25, 19:3). This seems to indicate that not all of the Baptist's disciples got the message about Jesus.

In Prison at the Whim of a Woman

In time, Herod Antipas, under pressure from Herodias, his consort, put the Baptist in prison (Luke 3:20). Josephus, the Jewish historian tells us that the prison was in the bleak fortress of Machaerus, which stood on a lonely ridge, surrounded by terrible ravines, overlooking the east side of the Dead Sea. It was one of the loneliest, grimmest and most unassailable fortresses in the world.

So John the Baptist, our free spirit, at home wandering in the desert, was confined in a dungeon. The bird was caged. The prophet was silenced after only a few months of very exciting and successful work. Instead of thousands thronging around him at Jordan, his only audience was Herod, who brought him out from time to time to talk with him. The Baptist kept telling Herod that it was not right for him to be married to his brother's wife (Mark 6:18).

The restriction of prison and the constant threat of death from Herodias must have been intolerable when the Baptist's work was hardly started. He had waited and prepared for 30 years and all he had was about six months' public ministry. Then, at the whim of a woman who did not like what he said, he was silenced, cooped up in a solitary cell.

News from Outside

His disciples visited him in prison and brought him news and especially the news about Jesus. We can reconstruct the content of these reports from the corresponding chapters in Matthew 4–10, Mark 1:14; 6:14 and Luke 4–7. When he heard that the Baptist was in prison, Jesus started to preach in Galilee. He called his disciples and began to teach them and the people what we know as the Sermon on the Mount. The Beatitudes on their own must have been hard for the Baptist to swallow, to say nothing about loving enemies and not judging people. He heard about lepers being healed, the demon-possessed man in the synagogue being delivered; the centurion's servant and the woman with the haemorrhage healed; Jairus' daughter raised from death, the paralysed man let down through the roof, forgiven and made to walk, the Gadarene demoniac delivered; it was all very puzzling for the Baptist.

Obviously, great things were happening and great power was being displayed, but where was it all leading, when Jesus taught such strange things? Why did he not visit the Baptist in prison and why could not some of his obvious power be exerted to get him out of prison.

John's Doubts

Doubts began to assail the Baptist. He was on the shelf with nothing to do. He was being greatly surpassed in popularity by another man. It did not seem as if what he had worked for was any nearer. No Kingdom of God being set up; no great wave of judgment instigated by the Messiah.

The last straw appears to have been the raising from the dead of the widow of Nain's son (Luke 7:11–17). The Baptist decided he had to get answers, so he sent two of his disciples to ask Jesus if he was the one John had said was going to come, or should they expect someone else? The Baptist was having doubts about Jesus. He was not sure now that Jesus was the Messiah. It must have been agony for him. It always is when doubts assail us and they do, even the choicest of God's servants.

The Baptist did the right thing. He voiced his doubts in the right direction. He took his doubts to Jesus himself. This was wise. Often doubt keeps us from the people and the practices that would help us; like prayer, the Bible, Christian friends. Keeping them to ourselves only compounds the problem. It is better to state the doubt and seek an answer from someone who can help, than to hide it in a shamefaced way.

Doubt is the normal accompaniment of developing faith. There are times when God allows us to be tested to prove our faith is in him alone. If doubt is not dealt with soon enough, then sometimes the questions become more important than the answers. This is a kind of intellectual hypochondria. Hypochondria is where the sickness becomes more important to the person than the cure. Hypochondriacs enjoy ill-health. John was wise to send to Jesus and state his doubt and his fear.

Jesus' Answer

Jesus, when he had heard the Baptist's question, seems to have gone on doing the same things the Baptist had been hearing about. Then he told John's disciples to report back to him what they had seen and heard. He couched his reply in words that the Baptist would recognize from Isaiah, his favourite prophet. 'The blind will be able to see, and the deaf will hear. The lame will leap and dance, and those who cannot speak will shout for joy' (Isaiah 35:5). 'The Sovereign LORD has filled me with his Spirit. He has chosen me and sent me to bring good news to the poor' (Isaiah 61:1).

In effect, Jesus was saying, 'What I am doing is consistent with the prophecies about Messiah.' It was a biblical answer. He was showing the Baptist, as he later showed his own disciples, that the place to turn to in doubt was the scriptures (Luke 24:27). We need to note that Jesus did not himself go to the Baptist or work for his release. In the quotation from Isaiah 61, he leaves out the second half of the text which speaks of announcing release to the captives and freedom to those in prison.

We do not know whether John was reassured or not. We might think that if we had been the Baptist, the answers his disciples brought, might have served only to raise more questions. Yet, this is all the answer that the Baptist was given. What Jesus was doing fitted the prophecies about Messiah. He then adds a rather negative postscript. 'How happy are those who have no doubts about me!'

It sounds like a sting in the tail. It could be just a sad reflection, a sigh of regret that a valued friend was finding difficulty understanding his role. It has often happened. Savonarola (1452–1498), the fiery Italian reformer, wavered in prison in Florence and was executed for heresy. Jerome of Prague, (1371–1416) the Bohemian reformer was clapped in prison in Constance and had his doubts there before he was burnt as a heretic. Luther was a man whose courage, like that of the Baptist, had enabled them to stand unquailing before angry councils and threatening kings. Although he survived the restriction placed on him in the castle at Wartburg, he had fantasies there which agitated and tortured his ardent spirit.

Jesus' Estimate of John

As the Baptist's disciples left, Jesus began to speak to the people about him. It is as though, having said something that was open to more than one interpretation, he wanted to correct any false impression that John had fallen in his estimation.

He threw a caustic question to the bystanders, among whom were many who had gone out to hear the Baptist preach and see him baptising people at the river Jordan, 'When you went out to John in the desert, what did you expect to see? A blade of grass bending in the wind? What did you go out to see? A man dressed up in fancy clothes?' It was a rhetorical question expecting the answer 'No!' it was so ridiculous.

He then answers it himself. 'People who dress like that and live in luxury are found in palaces!' He then follows that with a genuine challenge to tell him, whether they did not really go out to see and hear an austere, genuine prophet. Assuming their agreement, he pursues the subject and gives his own verdict. 'Yes indeed, but you saw much more than a prophet.' He goes on to affirm his own endorsement and enhancement of their view, saying that the Baptist was the person foretold by the prophets Malachi and Isaiah who would precede and prepare the way for Messiah. In fact, he told them that the Baptist was the greatest prophet who ever lived.

The Baptist and The Kingdom of God

Both John and Jesus said, 'Repent for the Kingdom of God is near!' (Matt. 3:2, 4:17). In this incident it became clear that the Baptist had a different idea of the kingdom from Jesus. Jesus underlined that when he spoke to the people. He told them that there had been from the Baptist's time a powerful movement towards the kingdom of God. The movement had derived its initial impetus from John the Baptist. No one could have done it better, but he was the end of a line, starting with Moses, including Elijah and right up to Malachi. Having said that, Jesus takes the opportunity to give new substance to the only other title that Jesus was given at his birth, a **'King like David'** (Luke 1:32). He makes it clear that John is the end of a line and the Kingdom is something different and still to be inaugurated.

Jesus implies that John was not in the Kingdom and so the least person who was really in the Kingdom, had a great advantage over the Baptist. The moral sternness of the Baptist was his greatness and also his weakness. It led him to doubt Jesus and made him a contrast to rather than an example of what the Kingdom of God was about (Luke 7:28).

Jesus then directed his remarks to the crowd. He said they were like two groups of children who kept disagreeing about what game they would all play. They called the Baptist mad because he was so austere. They called Jesus himself a glutton and a drunkard, because he ate and drank normally and kept company that they disapproved of. In other words, they sat on the fence and did not respond to either, but time would show the truth of the matter.

The Baptist's role, then was twofold. He showed who Messiah was and what the Kingdom was not. This was no doubt hard for the Baptist to bear in the darkness of his prison, especially when he was not given the encouragement of the positive things Jesus said about him. We do not always know how positive God is about us. It may only be at the end that we will hear, 'Well done, good and faithful servant.'

20

John the Baptist's Death

The Ultimate Foreshadowing

Matthew 14:1–12, Mark 6:14–19
Luke 9:7–9

The messengers returned with Jesus' answer
to the Baptist's question. We do not know if
John was assured by it or not, for there is no
further word from him. Herod had a birthday
soon after, and the Baptist was executed. It is
a tragic story.

Birthday Nemesis
What a scene it was! Herod had arranged for
celebrations on his birthday, either at
Machaerus or some neighbouring palace. All
the chief government officials, the military
commanders, and the leading citizens of
Galilee were invited to his party. We can
imagine the extravagant display. Nothing
would be missing which wealth or royalty
could procure. But Herodias had craftily
provided the king with an unexpected and

exciting pleasure. The banquet was over. The guests were full of food and flushed with wine. Salome herself, the daughter of Herodias, was in the prime of her young and lustrous beauty. She came in and danced, and pleased Herod and his guests. So the king said to the girl, in the delirium of his drunken approval, 'What would you like to have? I will give you anything you want.' With many vows he said to her, 'I swear that I will give you anything you ask for, even as much as half my kingdom!'

The girl went out and asked her mother, 'What shall I ask for?' It was exactly what Herodias expected. She might have asked for robes, or jewels, or palaces, or whatever a woman like her loves. But to a mind like hers, revenge was sweeter than wealth or pride. We may imagine with what fierce malice Herodias hissed out the answer, 'The head of John the Baptist.' The girl hurried back at once to the king and demanded imperiously, 'I want you to give me here and now the head of John the Baptist on a dish!'

Did Herodias think her petition would be received with a burst of laughter? If so, she was disappointed. This made the king very sad, but he could not refuse her because of the vows he had made in front of all his guests. So at once, he sent off a guard with orders to bring John's head. The guard left, went to the prison, and cut John's head off; then he brought it on a dish and gave it to the girl, who gave it to her mother.

Here is where the nemesis comes in. The man who has played with John the Baptist, hearing and turning away repeatedly is now caught in the net of the lust that John had condemned. What had originally swept him into the arms of Herodias now swept him to become John's reluctant but inevitable executioner. Herodias knew her man and engineered it to perfection. The main dish at the birthday party turned out to be the first martyr of the faith of Christ.

The Baptist is Mourned

Tradition tells us that Herodias ordered the headless trunk to be flung over the battlements of the fortress for the dogs and vultures to devour. The gospel record is that 'John's disciples came, carried away his body, and buried it; then they went and told Jesus.' When Jesus heard it, his instinct was to get away to a place by himself. We can understand. It was a solemn moment. When the people caught up with him, Mark says he saw them as sheep without a shepherd (Mark 6:34). and his heart was filled with pity for them. Was he thinking of John?

Herod's Remorse

Later, when the reputation of Jesus began to spread everywhere, Herod heard about it. Some people were saying, 'John the Baptist has come back to life! That is why he has this power to perform miracles.' Others said, 'He is Elijah'. Others said, 'He is a prophet, like one of the prophets of long ago.' When Herod heard it, he said, 'He is John the Baptist! I had his head cut off, but he has come back to life!' What he had done haunted him for the rest of his life

The True Forerunner

There is a parable here. John the Baptist had sounded warnings of terrible judgment with the voice of a trumpet in the ears of thousands. He ends up as a victim of as grizzly an end as can be imagined. And yet it was not a setback. If anything it was a model. The world is to be won by victims who are faithful unto death, more than by victors who are always blooming in life.

We note that, just before his last journey to Jerusalem, Jesus went back to where John had baptized (John 10:40–41). There was still talk there about John two years later. We have the feeling that Jesus was preparing himself for what was to come to him. It was here he delayed two days before responding to the desperate pleas of Martha and Mary to come and heal their brother Lazarus who was sick. He needed time to draw strength from the memory of John.

We know that he was still comparing himself and his reception with the Baptist's in the last week of his life. He was challenged about the authority by which he acted. His response was to ask them about John the Baptist and his authority, obviously feeling it was going the same way for him. So where Peter and the others were of little help to him in his trial and suffering, the memory of John was there to strengthen him. We have the feeling also that John's shadow is around, when Jesus is taken before Herod and remains in stony silence. He knew what to expect from John's executioner. There was nothing to be said.

So John not only modelled the kingdom in his clothing and food. He modelled it in his death. Even before the cross, he demonstrated the truth of the corn of wheat that has to fall into the ground and die if there is to be any fruit.

The First Beacon of the Kingdom

Jesus said to the Jews in Jerusalem that John the Baptist was a lamp burning and shining (John 5:35). He was the herald of the dawn. Mark, Luke and John get him into their very first chapter. Matthew makes it clear that Jesus' public ministry began with the Baptist.

When they are looking for an apostle to replace Judas, it has to be someone who went back as far as the Baptism of John. In sermons in Acts John the Baptist is again the starting point for talking about Jesus (Acts 10:37, 13:24–25). We have seen just how bright a light he was. 'Yet', says John, the apostle, 'he was not the light. He came to tell about the light.'

Summary

The Baptist's achievements are well summed up in the words of Luke, with one word change. 'Peoples' hopes began to rise and they began to wonder whether John perhaps might be the Messiah' (Luke 3:15). He did this by modelling an arresting, alternative lifestyle. He held a microphone to the people's hopes and fears. He was open to God and announced progressively what God told him about Messiah. He put into words perceptions that people knew but could not state. If we make a list of these, they were:

- The pointlessness of their ethnic pride as children of Abraham.
- The emptiness of merely formal religion. Baptism needs to be accompanied by a change of heart and behaviour.
- Greed benefits no one in the long run,

whether in the people, the tax collectors or the soldiers.

- The use of power or privilege for personal indulgence was sick, as Herod showed.
- People need genuine and lasting inward change.
- Doom is inevitable if there is no U-turn from sin.

Having got people to put a name to their hopes and fears, and to wonder if there might not be an answer, they were ready for Jesus who then came to put God's grace to the forefront instead of his judgment.

Appendix 1

The Virgin Birth

The material in the book rests on the belief that Jesus was purposefully born of the Virgin Mary by the direct intervention of the Holy Spirit without a human father. Since those who read it are likely to meet people who confidently assert that this is a myth, I am adding this appendix to present the grounds on which I accept the virgin birth as a fact of history. To begin, let us follow the pattern and look at what the gospels say.

A Unique Birth for a Unique Person

The writers of the gospels were conscious from the beginning that they were describing a unique event. Matthew says that the angel told Joseph in his dream, 'Joseph, ... do not be afraid to take Mary to be your wife. For it is by the Holy Spirit that she has conceived' (Matt. 1:20). Luke says that the angel told Mary, 'The Holy Spirit will come on you, and God's power will rest upon you. For this reason the holy child will be called the Son of God.' John clinches what the others describe when he calls Jesus 'the only begotten son of God' (John 1:14,17, 3:16 AV). It is surprising, therefore, when critics argue that it could not have happened because there are no parallels, when that is what the writers say about it.

Others assert that it must be a myth because there are parallels in other religions. Yet, when you look at these there are more differences than similarities in the ones that are cited. The Buddha, for example, was said to be born when a white elephant entered the side of his mother while she was asleep, and she conceived. This Buddhist legend arose hundreds of years after Gautama Buddha was dead, not within the lifetime of his family. It is obviously legendary or dreamlike in a way that the Gospel accounts are not. Such pagan myths were anathema to Jews and the idea that the very Jewish Matthew could have imitated some pagan myth in this way seems wholly unlikely.

As Impossible Then as Now

The people involved in the Nativity thought that, humanly speaking, birth without a human father was impossible. Mary said, 'I am a virgin. How, then, can this be?' The angel responded, 'There is nothing that God cannot do' (Luke 1: 34, 37). Joseph and Mary had as much difficulty in believing in the possibility we have today. Even with science at a much lower level that we have reached today, birth from a virgin without a man was as impossible then as now. This has not changed with the greater sophistication in biology.

Two Separate Accounts

On close reading, the accounts in Matthew and Luke are different both in substance and character. Matthew pays more attention to the Joseph side of the story. Luke tells us much more about Mary and her kinsfolk. The two accounts are not, however, contradictory, If there are two distinct accounts of the virgin birth, which do not contradict each other, the basic fact that such a birth occurred becomes more, not less, likely.

The birth stories are of a piece with the rest of the gospels, which they begin. The credibility that attaches to the rest of the gospels cannot be withheld from the early chapters, especially in the case of Luke who says that he researched everything carefully (Luke 1:1–4).

Matthew and Luke are believed to have been written in the third quarter of the first century. This means that there would be people alive who could have denied that these birth stories were true. There was no credible denial or any alternative suggested. True, there was a suggestion that Jesus was an illegitimate child as is hinted by the Pharisees, 'We be not born of fornication!' (John 8:41 AV) That explanation, however, was from the beginning seen to be the likely slur on the character of Mary and more a corroboration of the event as told by the gospel writer (Matt. 1:19).

The Science of it

I am not a scientist but there are two quotes that have helped me and they speak for themselves. Prof. George Romanes was Regius Professor of Physics at Oxford and reckoned to be Charles Darwin's greatest disciple. In a book published in 1904, *Thoughts on Religion* (pp.174–176) he said:

> The doctrine of the incarnation seemed to me most absurd in my agnostic days. But now as a pure agnostic (one without prejudices) I see no rational difficulty at all. At one time it seemed to me that no proposition, verbally intelligible as such, could be more violently absurd than this doctrine of the Incarnation. Now I see that this point is wholly unrational, due to the blindness of reason itself, promoted by scientific habits of thought.
>
> What lies behind the reluctance to believe such a birth? It seems to be inconsistent with the ordered universe of science. But this universe of science is not the real universe. It is only an abstraction, a section cut off, a mode made for working purposes. In my 70 years of life, I have

seen three such models created and abandoned... You cannot stake your life on two such instabilities as a changing science and a growing mind. This is to build your house on the sands. The real world includes God, the Beautiful, the True, Relationships as well as existences. Science by itself cannot judge the Truth because it is not its province.

When the Virgin Birth is denied for scientific reasons, it is a most unscientific procedure. It is a statement of faith (or rather unbelief) that there is nothing more than observed data. It goes along with the rejection of special creation.

Forty three years later C. S. Lewis says in his Book, *Miracles*, (1947, pp.50–52):

You will hear people say, 'The early Christians believed that Christ was the son of a virgin, but we know that this is a scientific impossibility'. Such people seem to have an idea that belief in miracles arose at a period when men were so ignorant of the course of nature that they did not perceive a miracle to be contrary to it. A moment's thought shows this to be nonsense: and the story of the Virgin Birth is a particularly striking example.

When St Joseph discovered that his fiancée was going to have a baby, he not unnaturally decided to repudiate her. Why? Because he knew just as well as any modern gynaecologist that in the ordinary course of nature Women do not have babies unless they have lain with men. No doubt the modern gynaecologist knows several things about birth and begetting which St Joseph did not know. But those things do not concern the main point, that a virgin birth is contrary to the course of nature. St Joseph obviously knew that. In any sense in which it is true to say now, 'The thing is scientifically impossible,' he would have said the same. The thing always was, and was always known to be, impossible unless the regular processes of nature were, in this particular case, being overruled or supplemented by something from beyond nature.

When St Joseph finally accepted the view that his fiancée's pregnancy was due not to unchastity but to a miracle, he accepted the miracle as something contrary to the known order of nature....... When a thing professes from the very outset to be a unique invasion of nature by something from outside, increasing knowledge of Nature can never make it either more or less credible than it was at the beginning........ The grounds for belief and disbelief are the same today as they were two thousand, or ten thousand years ago. If St Joseph had lacked faith to trust God or humility to perceive the holiness of his spouse, he could have disbelieved in the miraculous origin of her Son as easily as any modern man; and any modern man who believes in God can accept the miracle as easily as St Joseph did...

It Makes Sense

Given that the recovery of sinful, fallen humanity was the project, the manner of Jesus' birth fits in nearly every way.

It fits philosophically and doctrinally. The person needed for this task had to be divine and sinless. A God who cannot intervene, cannot save. The Virgin Birth tells us that the Son of God came into history. Karl Barth makes the point that Christ by his virgin birth avoids our sin-inheritance, but by the same Virgin Birth, takes on our creatureliness. He is not mere man; he is not mere God. He is the true God-man who is all that God is and at the same time all that man is, sin apart, born not of blood, nor of the will of the flesh, nor of the will of man but of God.

It fits ethically. Mary's consent was sought to take on her role. It involved her believing and co-operating. It was a voluntary act on her part. Does it not fit, that the Spirit who breathed into man to make him a living soul, in God's image, should overshadow a humble virgin and create in her a second Adam to save the first. Could he not also, by virtue of his person and work for us, in turn be able bring us a new birth to transform us into his image that was the original intention.

It fits personally. It opens up the possibility that we might have a new birth. By an act of God the Holy Spirit, we can become partakers of the divine nature, not by blood, nor of the will of the flesh, nor of the will of man, but of God. Yes, it fits. The subject is not one of mere academic interest. It is part of that total work of God in Christ that opens up for us a way in which we, by the same Spirit by whom he was conceived, might come to plant within us his own nature that might, by his grace, grow into complete likeness to him.

Appendix 2

Preaching on Bible Characters

The aims in preaching on Bible Characters

1. **Short term:**

    1. To get the attention of the congregation.

    2. To get across a truth of the gospel.

    3. To tell it in their language (Family Talk/ Popular Psychology).

    4. To start post service conversations.

2. **Long Term:**

    1. To fill in people's knowledge of the Bible story. (Biblical Literacy) like painting by numbers.

    2. To give them help with everyday problems, relationships and conduct. and a means of talking about these things with others.

Tips on how to do it from scratch

1. Do your own basic work on the text. There is a lot more there than we have noticed, so, this means going over it in detail to get all the elements of the 'story'. (One way of doing this is to write out the passage taking a new line for each phrase or thought.) Pay attention to the relationships of the person to their family, parents, brothers, sisters, children, and to others in the story. Note the answers to the questions, Where? How far? When? How long? Who? What actually happened in what order?

2. Check all the other references to the person in a Bible Concordance and see what that search yields in the way of background or additional detail.

3. Look up details in a Bible Dictionary.

4. Consult the commentaries for what they say about the person, not so much about the text.

3. Use your imagination! Try to experience and tell the story from the point of view of the main characters in the story.

4. Let it fall into episodes or chapters that will

be easy to follow and that build up to one or two main points.

5. Think of illustrations from your own experiences or from biographies, books, magazines or newspapers that you have read.

6. Do a detailed outline or write it out in full but....

7. Tell it as a story. (*Story Telling: A Practical Guide.* by Lance Pierson S.U.)

8. One tip on using a character from this book. You need to contextualise what is in the chapter to the place, the time, the people and the occasion when you are to preach it. This usually means:

   1. Reworking how you open and close the sermon to fit the occasion and audience.

   2. Omitting sections that do not apply or would be strange to your audience.

   3. Substituting or adding new illustrations that would speak to your audience.

Christian Focus Publications
publishes books for all ages:

Our mission statement: -

STAYING FAITHFUL
In dependence upon God we seek to help make his infallible word, the Bible, relevant. Our aim is to ensure that the Lord Jesus Christ is presented as the only hope to obtain forgiveness of sin, live a useful life and look forward to heaven with him.

REACHING OUT
Christ's last command requires us to reach out to our world with his gospel. We seek to help fulfill that by publishing books that point people towards Jesus and for them to develop a Christ-like maturity. We aim to equip all levels of readers for life, work ministry and mission.

Books in our adult range are published in three imprints.

Christian Heritage contains classic writings from the past.

Mentor focuses on books written at a level suitable for Bible College and seminary students, pastors, and other serious readers; the imprint includes commentaries, doctrinal studies, examination of current issues, and church history.

Christian Focus contains popular works including biographies, commentaries, basic doctrine, and Christian living. Our children's books are also published in this imprint.

For a free catalogue of all our titles, please write to:

Christian Focus Publications, Geanies House, Fearn
Ross-shire, IV20 1TW, Scotland

www.christianfocus.com